A Close-Up Look At Digging Into Dinosaurs

L ooking at your Table of Contents, you can see we've divided the study of dinosaurs into five main sections, followed by a craft section and the Appendix.

Each of the first five sections includes *background information* to explain concepts and vocabulary, *activities* that relate to the section theme, and *Copycat Pages* that reinforce many of the concepts in the activities.

You can choose single activity ideas or teach each section as a unit. Either way, each activity stands by itself and includes teaching objectives, materials needed, suggested age levels, subjects covered, and a step-by-step explanation of how to do the activity. (The objectives, materials, age levels, and subjects are highlighted in the left-hand margin for easy reference.)

AGE GROUPS

The suggested age groups are:
- Primary (grades K-2)
- Intermediate (grades 3-5)
- Advanced (grades 6-8)

Each chapter begins with primary activities and ends with intermediate or advanced activities. But don't feel bound by the grade levels we suggest. You'll be able to adapt many of the activities to fit your particular age group and needs.

OUTDOOR ACTIVITIES

Although you won't see dinosaurs roaming in the wild, you can still take your group outside for some dinosaur-related activities. Outdoor activities are coded in the chapters in which they appear with this symbol:

COPYCAT PAGES

The *Copycat Pages* supplement the activities and include ready-to-copy games, puzzles, coloring pages, worksheets, and mazes. *Answers to all Copycat Pages are on page 64.*

WHAT'S AT THE END

The sixth section, *Crafty Corner,* will give you some art and craft ideas that complement many of the activities in the first five sections. And the last section, the *Appendix,* is loaded with reference suggestions that include books, records, and films. The Appendix also has dinosaur questions and answers, background information about dinosaur mysteries, and a chart listing dinosaur sizes and other information.

DINOSAUR NAMES IN PRINT

As you read through *Digging into Dinosaurs*, you will see that we used two styles in naming dinosaurs—capitalized in italic type or lower case in regular type. No, we're not confused or being inconsistent. It's just that the first style is always used when referring to a dinosaur's (or any other animal's or plant's) genus and species, such as *Tyrannosaurus rex*, or when referring only to the genus, *Tyrannosaurus*. When a common or general name for a dinosaur is used, the scientific name is often modified and the capitalization and italics are dropped. For example, "Look at that *Tyrannosaurus*" becomes "Look at that tyrannosaur."

WHY DINOSAUR NAMES AND FACTS KEEP CHANGING

Paleontologists know a lot about dinosaurs. But there's also a lot they don't know. One of the problems in studying dinosaurs is that there are only a limited number of fossils to study.

So far, about 300 different kinds of dinosaurs have been discovered and named. But with some, only one or two specimens have been found. And that sometimes means a piece of bone or tooth is all there is to study.

So without much to go on, scientists must try to figure out what kind of dinosaur it was, what it was related to, and what it looked like.

When more information turns up, the old information may not seem quite right. And so information is constantly being updated. That's why, for example, the name *Brontosaurus* (one of the most well-known dinosaurs of all) was changed to *Apatosaurus*. Paleontologists used to think these dinosaurs were two separate species. But when new evidence turned up, they decided *Apatosaurus* and *Brontosaurus* were the same creature. And because *Apatosaurus* had been named first, it is now considered the correct name to go by.

Besides name differences, you will find discrepancies from one book to another on the pronunciation of dinosaur names, measurements given for body parts, and even descriptions of how the dinosaurs lived. There are two main reasons for the discrepancies. One is that paleontologists disagree on how fossil evidence should be interpreted and how to pronounce dinosaur names. The other reason is that once a book is written it becomes out-of-date almost immediately. And new books with more up-to-date information conflict with old hypotheses and arguments.

In *Digging into Dinosaurs*, we relied on many current dinosaur reference books and our scientific consultant, Dr. Philip Currie, to make sure our information is as current and accurate as possible.

TABLE OF CONTENTS

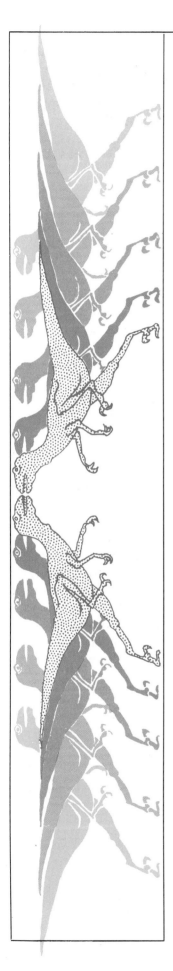

WHAT MAKES A DINOSAUR A DINOSAUR?

T wo hundred million years ago the earth was much different from what it is today. In most areas, the climate was warm and mild. A shallow sea stretched across the middle and southern parts of what would become North America. The Rocky Mountains hadn't formed yet, and flowering plants were just beginning to grow among the lush ferns and cycads. Tiny shrewlike mammals scurried in the undergrowth, along with quick-footed lizards. But by far the most dynamic and dominant land animals at this time were the dinosaurs.

What Was a Dinosaur?

Dinosaurs were a special group of prehistoric reptiles that lived during the *Mesozoic Era,* which lasted for almost 180 million years, from 245 million years before present (B.P.) to 65 million years B.P. Some dinosaurs were huge—over 15 times the size of an elephant. Others were smaller than a rooster.

All dinosaurs seem to have lived on land. Some ran around on their hind legs and others clomped along on all fours. Some were meat eaters that hunted alone or in packs. Others were plant eaters that often grazed in herds as cows and deer do today.

Although many dinosaurs wandered into swamps, marshes, and lakes for food and water, none were totally aquatic. And no dinosaur has yet been discovered that could fly.

Which Animals Were Not Dinosaurs?

Many prehistoric animals were not dinosaurs, including many of the prehistoric reptiles. These non-dinosaur animals included: flying reptiles (pterosaurs); giant aquatic creatures such as the plesiosaurs, giant sea turtles, and huge prehistoric crocodiles; primitive sail-back reptiles such as *Dimetrodon*; and saber-toothed cats and woolly mammoths (mammals that lived long after the dinosaurs had become extinct). See "Who's a Dinosaur" on page 12.

Where Did the Word "Dinosaur" Come From?

In 1674, the first dinosaur bone was discovered in southern England. But it wasn't until 1841 that the word "dinosaur" was invented.

Richard Owen, an English scientist, had been carefully studying the ancient reptile bones that had been dug up in England. After comparing them to modern animal bones, he decided they were very different from those of any reptile he had ever seen or studied. He thought they belonged to huge, extinct, lizardlike creatures that were probably ferocious because of their enormous sizes. So he called this new group of extinct reptiles "dinosaurs," which comes from two Greek words meaning "terrible lizards." Today we know the dinosaurs were not lizards at all. They were an altogether different group of reptiles, and many of them were far from terrible.

How Do Dinosaurs Compare with Other Animals?

Most scientists think that dinosaurs were reptiles because they have many reptilian characteristics, such as:
• *Reptilelike skulls* (Many dinosaur skulls resemble those of present-day reptiles.)
• *Eggs* (Many dinosaurs laid eggs, just as modern reptiles do.)

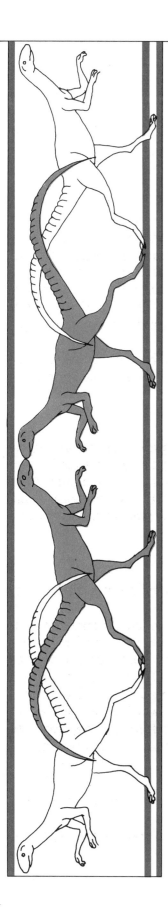

- *Cold-bloodedness* (Many scientists think that at least some of the dinosaurs, if not all of them, were cold-blooded and so were not able to control their internal body temperatures. Lizards, turtles, crocodiles, and snakes are also cold-blooded.)

But many scientists think that dinosaurs were very advanced reptiles because they had some characteristics that were similar to those of birds and mammals, such as:

- *Parental care* (Some of the dinosaurs cared for their babies long after they hatched, just as most birds and mammals do.)
- *Feeding behavior* (Many dinosaurs hunted in packs or grazed in herds, just as many mammals do.)
- *Warm-bloodedness* (Just as some scientists think dinosaurs were cold-blooded, others think all or some of them were warm-blooded, as birds and mammals are. See page 57 in the Appendix for more about this.)

How Were Dinosaurs Different from Other Reptiles?

Dinosaurs had many characteristics that are similar to those found in other reptiles. But they also had some characteristics that seem to be unique. For example, if you could have watched a dinosaur walk, you would have seen that it moved differently from a turtle, crocodile, or lizard. Most dinosaurs walked with their legs under their bodies for support, which raised them above the ground. But lizards, crocodiles, and turtles move very close to the ground, with their legs sprawled out to the sides away from their bodies.

Some dinosaurs also had grasping hands, as people do. Unlike other reptiles, these dinosaurs would have been able to grasp and hold things, such as their prey.

But even though there are many differing characteristics, paleontologists still aren't exactly sure how dinosaurs fit in with and compare to other reptiles. There are many different opinions about how the dinosaurs were actually related to each other and to other prehistoric and modern animals.

How Dinosaurs Are Grouped

Since 1841, over 300 different kinds of dinosaurs have been discovered. After comparing skeletons and features, paleontologists have divided the dinosaurs into these two separate orders of reptiles: *lizard-hipped dinosaurs* (the saurischians) and *bird-hipped dinosaurs* (the ornithischians).

Lizard-hipped dinosaurs had hips (the bones of the pelvis) shaped like those of lizards. Some lizard-hipped dinosaurs, like the aggressive *Tyrannosaurus* and the smaller *Coelophysis*, were meat eaters. Others were plant eaters, like the gigantic *Apatosaurus* (also known as *Brontosaurus*) and its relatives.

Bird-hipped dinosaurs had hips that were similar to those of birds. Most bird-hipped dinosaurs were plant eaters. Many of them, like *Stegosaurus* and *Triceratops,* had strange horns, frills, spikes, scutes, or plates on their bodies.

As Big As . . .

Compare sizes of
dinosaurs to everyday
objects.

Objective:
*Name a dinosaur and
something in modern life
that is as big as the dinosaur.*

Ages:
Primary

Materials:
- *copies of page 13*
- *pictures of dinosaurs*
- *a basketball*
- *a golf club*

Subject:
Science

It's fun to imagine the lumbering giants of long ago that were bigger than a car, a bus, or even a building. But most kids are surprised to learn that some of the dinosaurs were as small as a cat or a bird.

Try this activity with your group to compare dinosaur dimensions to those of familiar objects. It's an easy way to help children picture how big the dinosaurs were.

First pass out copies of page 13 to all the kids and talk about the size comparisons on the page, one at a time. As you discuss the big dinosaur, for example, show the kids pictures of *Apatosaurus* (it used to be called *Brontosaurus*), *Diplodocus,* or any of the other large dinosaurs known as *sauropods*. (The sauropods were large, plant-eating dinosaurs.) Explain that, despite their size, these big beasts were not aggressive hunters. Instead, they spent most of their time grazing on plants.

Next have the group look at the picture of the dinosaur egg on their sheets. Explain that some dinosaur eggs were about as big as a basketball—nearly twice the size of an ostrich egg. Tell them an egg this size could have made an omelet for 15 or more people! Hold up a basketball to help the children visualize just how large some dinosaur eggs were.

Now show the kids a picture of the horned dinosaur known as *Triceratops.* Have them look at their sheets to see that this dinosaur's brow horns were nearly as long as they (the children) are tall. (Each brow horn was almost 3½ feet [1 m] long.) To make another *Triceratops* horn comparison, hold up a 4-foot (1.2-m) golf club. Have the kids take turns pretending to be a *Triceratops* by helping them hold the golf club against their foreheads. Then ask the group how *Triceratops* might have used its horns. (for fighting and protecting itself)

Next have the kids look at the picture of the dinosaur tracks. Explain that scientists have found tracks of all sizes. Some of the tracks are fairly small, but others are huge—big enough for a child to take a bath in!

Now have the children point to the picture of the *Tyrannosaurus* skull. Ask them what the picture above it is. (a calf) Explain that these huge dinosaurs had heads as big as a whole calf. Their huge jaws held lots of sharp teeth that the animals needed for hunting and eating.

The picture of the smallest dinosaur on the page, a *Compsognathus*, will probably come as a surprise to many of the children. *Compsognathus* is the smallest dinosaur yet discovered. (Some dinosaur babies are smaller, but *Compsognathus* is the smallest adult known.) If possible, show the children a picture of *Compsognathus*. Explain that it was about the size of a chicken. It had a long neck, a very long tail, and was a swift hunter. It chased lizards and other quick prey. Ask the kids if they can think of another way its ability to run fast could help *Compsognathus* survive. (The speedy dinosaur could run away from hungry enemies.)

As a follow-up activity, take an "As Big As" walk with your group. Before the walk, scout around your school or nature center so that you can locate some of the objects you'll be using as comparisons. (See pages 60 and 61 for a chart of measurements.)

On the walk itself, bring along some dinosaur pictures so you can remind the kids what some of the dinosaurs looked like. To get the group actively involved in the size comparisons, mark off the length of *Apatosaurus* (or some other dinosaur and its dimensions—see chart on page 8) and have the kids run the distance.

Sizing Up the Dinosaurs

Draw dinosaurs and other animals to scale.

Objectives:
Describe the range of dinosaur sizes. Compare dinosaur sizes to those of animals living today.

Ages:
Primary and Intermediate

Materials:
- *string or twine*
- *yarn (optional)*
- *felt-tipped markers*
- *pictures of dinosaurs*
- *chalk*

Subjects:
Science and Math

W hen most people think of dinosaurs, they think big— *huge,* even. But the sizes of dinosaurs actually ranged from animals weighing more than 50 tons (45 t) down to chicken-sized *Compsognathus.*

Your group can get a feel for the different sizes of dinosaurs by drawing these monstrous (and not so monstrous) animals lifesize on a hardtop playground or parking lot. Just make sure you have plenty of chalk on hand!

BEFORE YOU START

On page 8 we've listed four dinosaurs with their measurements. (If you need other dimensions, see the chart on pages 60 and 61 in the Appendix.) We've also included the dimensions of some modern-day giants so that your students can compare them to the dinosaurs. Before you begin this activity, measure your space so that you know how many drawings will fit.

HOW TO DO IT

Divide your group into teams and have the members of each team work together to complete a dinosaur or other animal drawing. Before heading out to the hardtop, give each team a picture of an animal and a list of its dimensions. Then let the kids practice drawing their animal's outline on paper. (Check the bibliography for good dinosaur reference books.) Next give each team a ball of string or twine, a felt-tipped marker, a ruler or yardstick, and several pieces of chalk. Tell the kids to bring their animal pictures and lists of dimensions out to the drawing area so they'll be able to refer to them.

Once outside, have the teams mark off their string in one-foot intervals, up to the length of their particular dinosaurs or modern-day animals. (Marking three-foot [1-m] intervals with a yardstick is faster for the really big dinosaurs.) Have the teams space themselves out to make room for all the beasts.

Next, have two members of each team stretch out the string to their beast's length. While those two stand there as markers, two other children can measure and mark the animal's height. You may want to have the kids chalk in lines for the length and height.

For easier drawing, have the kids first make an outline of the beasts' bodies with string or yarn. Then they can trace around the outline with their chalk. Let everyone have a chance to be artists by having the kids on the "ends" switch off with those doing the drawings. If you have a large group, let some of the kids in each team draw in part of their animal's environment. For example, the team working on *Apatosaurus* could add some leafy trees that this huge plant eater might browse on.

When all of the groups have finished their drawings, gather everyone into one large group. Tour all of the drawings,

Bruce Norfleet

letting each team tell about its beast. When you come to one of the really big dinosaur drawings—*Apatosaurus* or *Ultrasaurus*, for example—have a child lie down in the center of the drawing. Draw an outline of his or her body. You can also have the kids count off and walk, one by one, through the beast's mouth and down its throat. Starting with the tail, see how much of the dinosaur your group can fill up.

If you can't draw these large beasts outside, use brightly colored yarn to make the shape of a dinosaur right on the floor of your classroom or nature center. Have all the children lie inside the dinosaur; then read them a story about what life was like millions of years ago. (For younger kids, see "Annie Apatosaurus" on pages 26 27.)

Apatosaurus (*Brontosaurus*)
length: 70 feet (21 m) from tail to nose
shoulder height: 15 feet (4.5 m)
neck: 20 feet (6 m) long

Tyrannosaurus
length: 43 feet (13 m)
height: 18.5 feet (6 m)
head: 4 feet (1.2 m) long
jaws: 3 feet (90 cm) long
talons: 8 inches (20 cm) long
arms: 30 inches (76 cm) long

Ultrasaurus
length: 85 feet (26 m)
height: 45 feet (14 m)
front legs: 17 feet (5 m) long
neck: 20 feet (6 m) long
shoulder height: 25 feet (7.5 m)

Compsognathus
length: 2 feet (60 cm)
height: a little over a foot (30 cm)

Blue Whale
length: 100 feet (30 m)
height of back fin (dorsal): ½-1½ feet (15-45 cm)

Giraffe
length of legs: 6 feet (1.8 m)
height: 19 feet (6 m)
shoulder height: 11½ feet (3.5 m)

BRANCHING OUT: MATH

After sizing up the dinosaurs, make up some math problems for your group using prehistoric dimensions. Here are some ideas that you can adapt to fit the needs of your group:

If *Pteranodon* had a 27-foot (8.2-m) wingspread and the California condor has a 9-foot (2.6-m) wingspread, how many times larger was *Pteranodon*'s wingspread?

27 ÷ 9 = 3 times larger

Use the following facts to solve the egg problem below:

• The largest-known dinosaur eggs were laid by a dinosaur called *Hypselosaurus*. One of *Hypselosaurus*'s eggs could have made an omelet for 15 people!

• It takes about three chicken eggs to make an omelet for one hungry person.

About how many chicken eggs is one *Hypselosaurus* egg equal to?

15 x 3 = 45 chicken eggs

If the Flintstones really did eat dinosaur burgers, how many ¼ pounders could they have made from 50 tons of dinosaur meat?
50 tons x 2000 pounds (1 ton) = 100,000 pounds
100,000 pounds ÷ ¼ = 400,000 burgers

Dinosaur Facts and Fiction

Divide into teams and play a dinosaur question and answer game.

Objectives:
List three dinosaur facts. Give an example of a dinosaur misconception.

Ages:
Primary and Intermediate

Materials:
- *blackboard and chalk or markers and easel paper*
- *index cards or slips of paper*
- *list of dinosaur questions and answers (page 59 in the Appendix)*

Subject:
Science

There are a lot of misconceptions about dinosaurs. For example, many people think of dinosaurs as the biggest animals ever to live on earth.(The modern-day blue whale holds this record.) And a lot of people picture dinosaurs as slow-moving, dim-witted swamp dwellers.

Play this fact and fiction game with your group to clear up some of these dinosaur misunderstandings. You can also use this activity to introduce the subject of dinosaurs or to review what you have studied.

HOW TO SET UP THE GAME

1) Divide the group into two or more teams and have the kids in each team think up a team name. (For example, one team could be the Carnosaurs, one could be the Hadrosaurs, and another could be the Sauropods.)

2) Copy the picture of the dinosaur model below onto the chalkboard or onto a large piece of paper so that all the teams can see it. (Make sure to also include the numbers on each dinosaur part.)

3) Tape up large sheets of paper around the room (the size used on an easel) or use different sections of a chalkboard, making sure that each team has a place to draw. (Give each team a marker for the paper or chalk for the chalkboard.)

4) Copy the questions (page 59 in the Appendix) on slips of paper or index cards and put these in a paper sack or cardboard box. Add whatever questions you can think of.

THE OBJECT OF THE GAME

Explain that each team will be competing against the other teams to try to answer the most questions correctly. The object of the game is to be the *last* team to finish "building" the dinosaur. (If you use the game to introduce the subject of dinosaurs and the questions seem a bit difficult, try having the kids draw a piece of their dinosaurs each time they answer a question correctly. In this version of the game, the *first* team to finish building a dinosaur wins.)

DINOSAUR MODEL

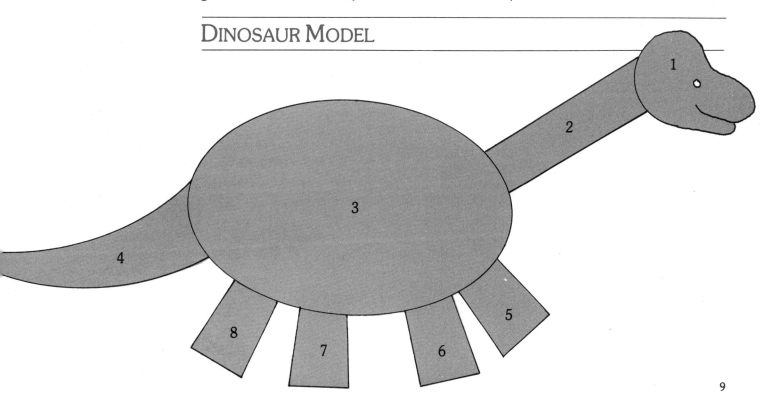

How To Play

Have a person from one team pick a question from the sack or box. (Alternate the question choosers from round to round.) Read the question and have each team get together in a huddle to decide on the answer. When all teams have finished tell each team to write their answer on a slip of paper. Then go from team to team and have them read their answers. Those teams that answer the question incorrectly must draw a dinosaur part on the board or on their easel paper. (Make sure all the teams can see each other's drawings.) The numbers on the model represent the order in which the parts should be drawn. For example, when a team incorrectly answers its first question, a representative from that team must draw the dinosaur's head. Use the same principle as in "Hangman": the team with the least-finished drawing at the end of the game wins.

After each question, discuss the answer. (We've listed questions in the Appendix. You can adapt the questions to make them easier or more difficult, depending on the needs of your group.)

Variations

1) You can make the game last longer by adding eyes, nostrils, mouth, toenails, and other features to the model.
2) Instead of asking all teams a question at the same time, you can alternate. Ask the first team a question, let them answer, and have them draw a part on the board if they miss. Then ask the next team a different question, and so on.

What's In A Name?

Alphabetize, spell, and make up dinosaur names. Create dinosaur tongue twisters.

Objectives:
Discuss two dinosaur names and what they mean. Describe how dinosaurs got their names.

Ages:
Primary, Intermediate, and Advanced

Materials:
- *copies of page 43*
- *paper and pencils*
- *crayons, markers, or colored pencils*
- *paste*
- *scissors*

Subjects:
Science and Language Arts

Children are fascinated with dinosaur names. Even before they can read they can pronounce such mouthfuls as *Apatosaurus, Diplodocus,* and *Styracosaurus.* As an introduction to dinosaurs or as a creative break, try some of these dinosaur "name games" and activities with your group.

Dinosaur A B Cs

To start this activity, ask the kids to name some of the dinosaurs they know. If they come up with several names write these on the board or a large piece of paper. (See the chart on pages 60 and 61 in the Appendix for correct spellings.) Then have the group alphabetize the names by asking them which name should be listed first, second, and so on.

Next pass out copies of page 43 . Go over the dinosaur names by having the kids pronounce each one as a group. Then have the kids alphabetize the names by cutting out the squares and pasting them on another sheet in the correct order. (For younger children, draw a grid on the board as a format for them to follow, numbering each square. You might also want the kids to draw their own grids before they paste down their dinosaur pictures.)

Name Wars

Many dinosaur names are hard to pronounce and harder to spell. Have a dinosaur spelling bee to familiarize your group with how dinosaur names are spelled.

First run off a list of the dinosaur names you want the group to try to learn. (The list should include pronunciations. See the chart on page 60 in the Appendix.) After everyone has had a chance to study the list, divide the group into two teams. Write the names and pronunciations on slips of paper and put them in a box. (Or just cut up the original study sheet.)

Next have one person from each team come up front. Pick a name from the box and pronounce it for the players. Then start with one of the two players and see if he or she can spell the name correctly. If the name is spelled correctly, the team gets ten points and two other players can come up for the next round. If the name is not spelled correctly, the person from the other team gets a try for nine points. Keep alternating until someone gets it right or you get down to zero points. Then have another pair come up. This time, start the spelling of a new word with the other team.

After each pair has had a turn, add up the points to see which team had the best spellers.

Note: Besides using dinosaur names, you can also use the words listed in the Glossary on page 58 or other dinosaur-related vocabulary words.

ORNILOPHOSAURUS

DINOSAUR TONGUE TWISTERS

This activity is just for fun. Pass out copies of page 43. Have each person pick one of the dinosaurs listed and find out a little about it. Then have everyone try to think up a crazy tongue twister with the dinosaur's name in it. Here is an example: Terrible-tempered *Tyrannosaurus* tears *Triceratops* into tough tidbits.

IT'S GREEK TO ME

Many dinosaurs have scientific names derived from Greek or Latin words. Others are named after special people or places. But all dinosaur names have Latinized endings, just as all other scientific animal and plant names do. For example, many dinosaur names end in "saurus." This is from the Greek word for lizard.

Write a list on the board of these Greek and Latin words and their English translations. Then have each person choose words from the list and make up two or three imaginary dinosaur names.

Now have the kids write the names and their meanings on a piece of paper without letting anyone else see what they've done. Collect their ideas and then make up a list of dinosaurs that includes some of their "fake" names along with real dinosaur names and meanings. (See the chart on page 60 in the Appendix for a list of dinosaur names.) Run off the name sheets and have each person circle the names of the dinosaurs that he or she thinks are real. As a follow-up, have the kids draw pictures of their imaginary dinosaurs. When they've finished drawing, have each child tell a little about his or her creation.

PREFIXES

aqua- (L) water
archi- (GR) primitive
brachio- (GR) arm
bronte- (GR) thunder
cory- (GR) helmet
di- (GR) two
dino- (GR) terrible
diplo- (GR) double
glyco- (GR) sweet
hetero- (GR) different
hexa- (GR) six
leuco- (GR) white
lopho- (GR) crest
micro- (GR) small
mono- (GR) one
myo- (GR) muscle
nodo- (L) knot
octa- (GR) eight

ops- (GR) face
optic- (GR) eye
orni- (GR) bird
pachy- (GR) thick
ped- (L) foot
phyto- (GR) plant
platy- (GR) flat
poly- (GR) many
proto- (GR) first
pteryg- (GR) wing
pyro- (GR) heat/fire
scolo- (GR) crooked
semi- (L) half
super- (L) above
terra- (L) land
tri- (GR) three
tyrannos- (GR) terrible
xeno- (GR) strange
xero- (GR) dry

SUFFIXES

-gnathus (GR) jaw
-mimus (GR) imitator
-saurus (GR) lizard

BOTH

-cephalic- (GR) head
-coel- (L) hollow/cavity
-derma- (GR) skin
-phil- (GR) loving
-odon- (GR) tooth

Put an X through the animals that *were not* dinosaurs. Circle the animals that *were* dinosaurs.

ANKYLOSAURUS

PTERANODON

PELONEUSTES

COELOPHYSIS

SABER-TOOTHED CAT

ARCHAEOPTERYX

STEGOSAURUS

DINICHTHYS

PARASAUROLOPHUS

PROTOCERATOPS

COPYCAT PAGE AS BIG AS . . . PICTURE SHEET

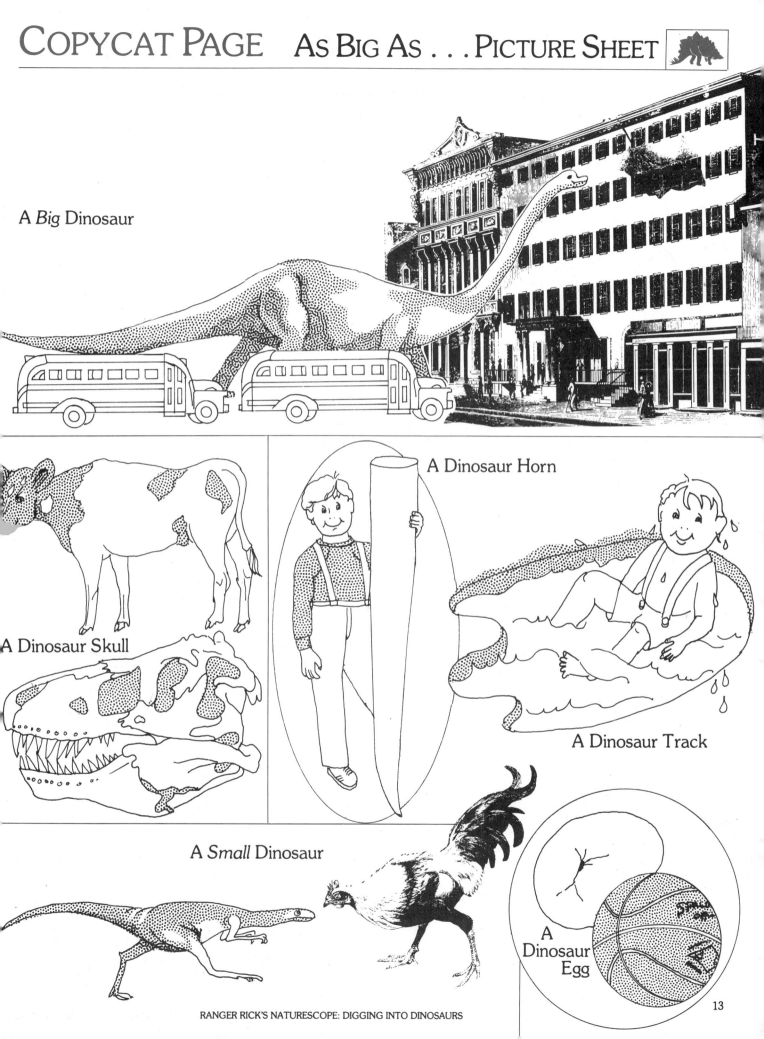

A *Big* Dinosaur

A Dinosaur Skull

A Dinosaur Horn

A Dinosaur Track

A *Small* Dinosaur

A Dinosaur Egg

GROWING UP AND STAYING ALIVE

f you took a time machine trip back to the Mesozoic Era, you would see a world alive with dinosaurs—searching for food, escaping from enemies, mating, drinking, resting—doing all the things wild animals do today. In the last 20 years, scientists have managed to piece together some exciting new ideas about how the dinosaurs really lived.

HATCHING OUT: Paleontologists think most dinosaurs hatched from eggs. Many of the eggs that have been found are fairly small. But others are over 10 inches (25 cm) long—twice the size of an ostrich egg. Even though a 10-inch egg is huge compared to the eggs we know today, it was not very big for a 33-ton (30-t) *Apatosaurus* or a 6-ton (5.5-t) *Triceratops*. But dinosaur eggs probably didn't get much bigger because the shells would have had to be very thick to support the weight of a giant egg. And that would have meant that no oxygen could have reached the baby dinosaur inside.

Nests: Dinosaur nests have been dug up in parts of Montana, southern France, Mongolia, Africa, Alberta, India, and China. (Some nests found in France are over 15 feet [4.5 m] wide!) These nests are similar to those of modern crocodiles and marine turtles. The fossilized eggs are clustered in piles of sand or mud. Paleontologists think many female dinosaurs dug nests with the claws on their feet.

Caring for the Young: Some paleontologists think many dinosaurs cared for their young long after hatching. They have found fossils of young dinosaurs clustered in their nests. These young were much older than a newly hatched baby. Paleontologists think the parents brought food back to the nest for their young. This is a characteristic of advanced animals such as mammals and birds.

HERDING: After studying thousands of dinosaur footprints and fossils, scientists think many of the plant-eating dinosaurs traveled in large herds for protection from enemies. Some also think young dinosaurs may have traveled in the center of the herds so that they were protected by the much larger and stronger adults on the outside. (Herds of elephants and some other animals do the same thing.)

Bone beds provide other clues that the dinosaurs traveled in herds. In some bone beds many skeletons from one kind of dinosaur are buried in the same place. In others, skeletons from several different kinds of dinosaurs are together. Some of these dinosaur burial grounds suggest that a terrible catastrophe, such as a flood or an earthquake, killed entire herds or groups of dinosaurs at once.

Many of the meat eaters also seem to have traveled in groups. Scientists now think that many of the carnivorous dinosaurs hunted in packs, as wolves do today.

MATING DISPLAYS: Many of the dinosaurs had strange-looking crests, frills, bumps, and spines on their heads, necks, and backs. Scientists think some of these odd parts were used in mating displays to attract members of the opposite sex.

The frills and crests might have become very colorful during the mating season, just as throat patches do in many lizards.

Scientists also think many of the males used their horns and thick skulls to fight for mates—just as bighorn sheep and other animals do today.

HOW LONG DID THEY LIVE? By comparing dinosaurs to animals living today, some scientists think that the largest individuals might have lived 200 years. Others think they might have lived even longer. But at this time no one knows for sure.

COLORS: Looking at a dinosaur skeleton, it's hard to tell what color the animal was. Many people once assumed dinosaurs were drab grays, greens, or browns. But now scientists think that some of them may have had bright stripes, spots, and patches, just as many lizards and snakes do today. Scientists also think the colors of some dinosaurs may have camouflaged them from enemies.

WERE THE DINOSAURS STUPID? Some of the dinosaurs were probably pretty slow "thinkers." Many had brains the size of a grapefruit in a body the size of two school buses.

But not all of the dinosaurs were as "dumb" as once thought. Many had brains that were large in proportion to their body weights. And scientists think the size of an animal's brain in proportion to the size of its body has much to do with its intelligence.

SPEED: Many of the dinosaurs were enormous and moved very slowly. (Scientists estimate that the large sauropods, such as *Brachiosaurus,* probably moved only about four miles [6 km] per hour.) Others were fast runners. *Struthiomimus* was one of the fastest dinosaurs. Some scientists think it could run over 50 miles (80 km) per hour.

Scientists estimate how fast the dinosaurs traveled by measuring the distance between fossilized tracks. (The faster an animal moves, the longer its stride.) Scientists also compare dinosaur skeletons with those of animals living today to get an idea about how fast dinosaur skeletons would have allowed their owners to move.

For their size, it's amazing just how fast some of the dinosaurs moved. For example, *Albertosaurus* weighed 2-3 tons (2-3 t), measured 36 feet (11 m) from its nose to its tail, and could probably run faster than a person can. Its strong legs had powerful muscles built for speed. *(continued next page)*

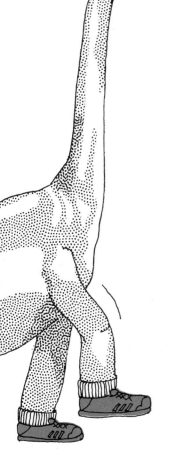

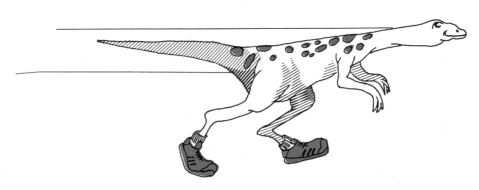

TEETH: Dinosaur teeth were different from those of mammals. Mammals have only two sets of teeth ("baby" teeth and permanent teeth). But dinosaurs—like other reptiles and like fishes—could keep replacing their teeth until they died. This meant that if a dinosaur broke a tooth or the tooth became worn down, another tooth would eventually grow in its place.

By studying fossilized teeth, scientists can tell whether a dinosaur ate plants, meat, or both. And they can also get an idea of the size of the dinosaur.

CLAWS AND HOOVES: Many of the large meat-eating dinosaurs had long, sharp claws on their hands and feet. (One fossilized claw was over 10 inches [25 cm] long!) These claws looked like the sharp talons of an eagle. They were used to capture large prey and hold it tight. Some of the smaller dinosaurs, such as *Deinonychus*, had a curved claw on each foot. Scientists think the owners of these sickle-like claws used them to rip open the bellies of their prey.

Some dinosaurs had bearlike claws. They used their claws to dig for insects and rip open logs and eggs. The fossilized "bear" claws of one dinosaur from Mongolia were more than three feet (0.9 m) long!

Scientists think the claws of the huge sauropods, such as *Apatosaurus*, were used for digging nests in the ground.

The duck-billed, horned, and armored dinosaurs had hooves—just as many animals do today. These hooves protected the ends of the toes.

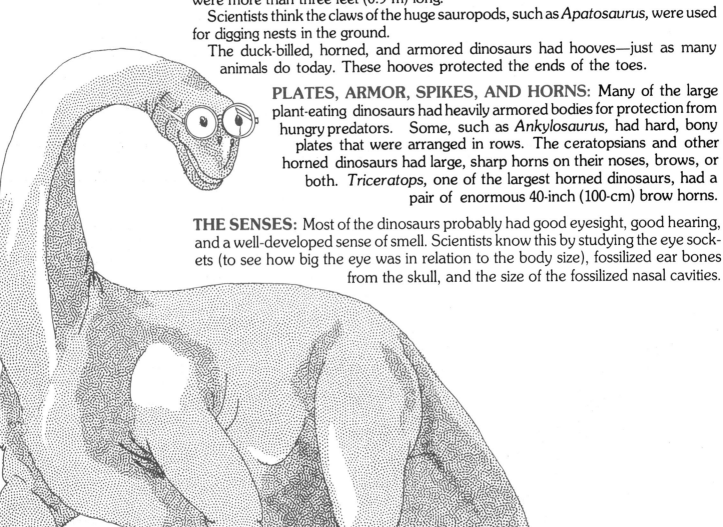

PLATES, ARMOR, SPIKES, AND HORNS: Many of the large plant-eating dinosaurs had heavily armored bodies for protection from hungry predators. Some, such as *Ankylosaurus*, had hard, bony plates that were arranged in rows. The ceratopsians and other horned dinosaurs had large, sharp horns on their noses, brows, or both. *Triceratops*, one of the largest horned dinosaurs, had a pair of enormous 40-inch (100-cm) brow horns.

THE SENSES: Most of the dinosaurs probably had good eyesight, good hearing, and a well-developed sense of smell. Scientists know this by studying the eye sockets (to see how big the eye was in relation to the body size), fossilized ear bones from the skull, and the size of the fossilized nasal cavities.

Prehistoric Parade

Sing a dinosaur song and perform the motions for each verse.

Objectives:
Name three dinosaurs and describe a characteristic of each.

Ages:
Primary

Materials:
- *pictures of dinosaurs*
- *guitar or piano (optional)*

Subjects:
Science and Music

inosaurs and other prehistoric reptiles came in all different shapes and sizes. Show your group pictures of *Tyrannosaurus, Stegosaurus, Hadrosaurus, Triceratops,* and a pterodactyl. (Check the bibliography for dinosaur picture books.)

Then go through each verse of the *Prehistoric Parade* (below) and teach your group the words and the sounds and motions that go with each verse. (It might be hard for younger children to learn the words. But they can still have fun with the sounds and motions.)

Sing the song to the tune of "When You're Happy and You Know It Clap Your Hands." You can adapt the movements and sounds any way that best fits your group. You can also have the group make up other verses to fit other prehistoric creatures. (After you sing the song, review the dinosaur characteristics and movements.)

PREHISTORIC PARADE

1. The dinosaurs once roamed throughout the land
   Throughout the land! [say it out loud]
   The dinosaurs once roamed throughout the land
   Throughout the land!
   It was oh, so long ago
   Now they're all extinct, you know
   The dinosaurs once roamed throughout the land.

2. *Tyrannosaurus* was a mighty beast
   Grrr-owl! [make growling sounds]
   Tyrannosaurus was a mighty beast
   Grrr-owl!
   It measured 40 feet
   Weighed six tons and gulped down meat
   Tyrannosaurus was a mighty beast.

3. *Stegosaurus* carried plates upon its back
   Clack, Clack [say it out loud and clap hands behind back]
   Stegosaurus carried plates upon its back
   Clack, Clack
   Its brain was very small
   It was hardly there at all!
   Stegosaurus carried plates upon its back.

4. *Hadrosaurus* could bellow, grunt, and snort
   Snort, Snort [make snorting, piglike sounds]
   Hadrosaurus could bellow, grunt, and snort
   Snort, Snort
   It munched on leaves and fruit
   With its funny, ducklike snoot
   Hadrosaurus could bellow, grunt, and snort.

5. *Triceratops* had three horns on its face
   Clash, Clash [say it out loud and put one fist over the other, covering nose]
   Triceratops had three horns on its face
   Clash, Clash
   Its enemies were few
   (They knew what those horns could do!)
   Triceratops had three horns on its face.

6. Pterodactyl glided through the sky
   Zoom, Zoom [say it out loud and hold arms straight out from sides]
   Pterodactyl glided through the sky
   Zoom, Zoom
   Not a bird or dinosaur
   But a reptile that could soar
   Pterodactyl glided through the sky.

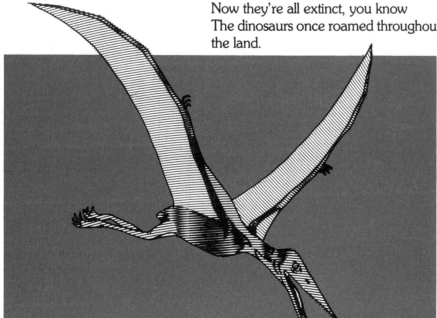

The Call of the Wild Dinosaurs

Invent dinosaur calls.

Objectives:
Invent the calls of several dinosaurs. Explain why dinosaurs made different kinds of calls.

Ages:
Primary and Intermediate

Materials:
- *pictures of dinosaurs*
- *dinosaur reference books*
- *tape recorder (optional)*

Subject:
Science

Here's an activity that will give your kids a chance to use their imaginations. It'll also get them thinking about how animals communicate through vocalizations.

Ask your group if they have any "noisy" pets. Have them imitate their pets' calls and ask them what they think the calls mean. Then explain to your group that many dinosaurs probably made noises too. And just like animals living today, they probably had different kinds of calls that had different meanings. For example, when a prairie dog is upset, it will often bark or whistle. But when greeting a fellow prairie dog, it will chatter and squeal. Many birds have special territory calls that say, "This is my area, keep off!" And they also have warning calls that say, "Watch out, here comes an enemy!"

In this "noisy" activity, your group will get to invent their own dinosaur calls. To start off, you might want to read this poem by X. J. Kennedy aloud:

Dinosaur Din

Did stegosaurus bellow like
A longhorn steer in Texas?
Could a songbird's tweet
Or twitter beat
Tyrannosaurus rex's?

Did pterodactyl cackle?
Did brachiosaurus bray?
Did monoclonius toot
Through his horny snoot
Ta ra ra boom de ay?

Did little lambeosaurus baa
Or did it bark in chorus?
Did the ankles clank
Like an army tank
On an ankylosaurus?

Today cars, planes and subway trains
Raise a whole lot of hullaballoo
But the rumble and roar
Of a dinosaur
I haven't once heard—have you?

X.J. Kennedy, "Dinosaur Din" from *The Phantom Ice Cream Man*. Copyright © 1975, 1977, 1978, 1979 by X.J. Kennedy. Reprinted by permission of Curtis Brown Ltd.

Now divide the group into teams and give each team a picture of a common dinosaur. Have the teams find out how their dinosaurs moved, what they ate, how they defended themselves, and where they lived. Then have them make up two calls for their dinosaurs. For example, the *Triceratops* team could make up a *Triceratops* warning call to warn other *Triceratops* that danger is near and a *Triceratops* mating call that the male might use to attract a female.

The calls can be bellows, squeaks, whistles, grunts, barks, screeches, or a combination of different sounds—whatever best fits the teams' particular dinosaurs. (Since this will be a noisy activity, you might want to do it outside.)

When the teams have finished making up their calls, have them stand up and give their calls to the other teams, one at a time. All the teams should tell something about their dinosaurs—and then explain how the dinosaurs used their calls. (You might want to have each team try to teach the calls to the other teams.)

As a variation, you can record the calls as the teams give them and play the calls back in a mixed-up order. See if the teams can guess which call goes with which dinosaur.

Beasts, Past and Present

Compare adaptations of dinosaurs and modern animals.

Objectives:
Name a dinosaur and an adaptation it has in common with a modern animal. Discuss how this adaptation helped the dinosaur survive and also helps the modern animal survive today.

Ages:
Primary

Materials:
- *pictures of dinosaurs*
- *copies of page 23*

Subject:
Science

Prehistoric animals had many of the same characteristics that animals have today. In this activity, your group will have a chance to compare dinosaurs and other prehistoric creatures with living animals by matching similar characteristics.

First pass out copies of page 23. Explain that each animal on the left has a special characteristic that one of the animals on the right also has. Have the kids try to match the animals that have common characteristics. (On some, there may be more than one match.)

After everyone is finished, discuss each match using the following information:
- *Giraffe and Apatosaurus:* With its long neck *Apatosaurus* could reach the highest leaves on the trees. Giraffes also munch on the highest leaves, using their long necks to reach them.
- *Lion and Tyrannosaurus: Tyrannosaurus* was a huge meat-eating dinosaur. It grabbed its prey and ripped it apart with its sharp teeth and claws. Lions are also predators with sharp teeth and claws.
- *Bighorn Sheep and Pachycephalosaurus: Pachycephalosaurus* is called a "thick-headed" dinosaur. That's because it had a nine-inch (22.5-cm)-thick bone on top of its skull. This bone helped to protect *Pachycephalosaurus's* brain. Just like bighorn rams today, this dinosaur butted heads with other males to win a mate.
- *Albatross and Pteranodon: Pteranodons* were huge flying reptiles. They had large, leathery wings and furry bodies. Like the albatrosses of today, they soared on the air currents, flapping only occasionally.
- *Rhinoceros and Triceratops: Triceratops* was a large, bulky plant eater with sharp horns on its snout and brows. It used its horns for fighting and for defending itself from enemies. Rhinos also have large horns on their snouts and will use their horns in much the same way.

After going over the Copycat Page, have the group try to think of other prehistoric animals that have something in common with animals today. Here are some examples:
- *Ankylosaurus* had a protective, armor-like covering similar to an armadillo's body covering.
- Hadrosaurs, sauropods, and other dinosaurs traveled in herds for protection, just as zebras, elephants, and deer do today.
- *Troodon,* like the cheetahs of today, hunted its prey by chasing it down.
- *Deinonychus* probably hunted in packs as wolves do today.

Now have the children look at their Copycat sheets again and see if they can find differences between the animals they connected. (For example, *Triceratops* was a reptile and a rhinoceros is a mammal.)

As a wrap-up, ask the children why they think animals from the past had some of the same characteristics and shapes as animals do today. (Special adaptations help all animals survive, and dinosaurs had the same needs that animals today have, such as finding food and protecting themselves from enemies.)

WHAT LIVED WHEN?

For younger children, pass out copies of page 21 for them to work on. When they've finished, talk about how, at the time of the dinosaurs, there were no cats or dogs, elephants or airplanes, or even people. But dinosaurs still had the same needs as animals living today have, such as finding food, water, and a place to lay eggs.

What sharp teeth we have!

All the Better to Eat With

Objectives:
Name one plant-eating and one meat-eating dinosaur. Describe how the skulls and teeth differ between these two types of animals. Name some modern-day plant eaters and meat eaters.

Ages:
Primary and Intermediate

Materials:
- *pictures of common plant-eating and meat-eating dinosaurs (see list in activity)*
- *copies of page 22*

Subject:
Science

W hat can you tell about a dinosaur from its skull? A lot! Scientists can tell if a dinosaur was an adult by looking at its teeth. They can estimate intelligence by measuring the braincase. And they can tell whether it was a meat eater or a plant eater by the size of the skull and the type of teeth in it.

If the skull of a dinosaur has powerful jaws and long pointed teeth, it's a good bet that the dinosaur was a hunter. But if the skull has flat, blunt teeth for grinding or chopping, then the dinosaur was probably a plant eater.

Lead a discussion with your group about the differences between plant-eating and meat-eating dinosaurs. If you have access to some skulls of modern-day animals, show these to the kids to start off the activity. Point out the sharp teeth of a typical meat eater, or carnivore. (A cat or fox skull is a good example.) Also show them the flat, blunt teeth of a plant eater, or herbivore. (A deer or cow skull will work well.)

Now use pictures to talk about dinosaur plant eaters and meat eaters. Hold up a picture of *Tyrannosaurus,* for example, to show the group a meat-eating dinosaur. Point out the huge jaws and the daggerlike teeth. A dinosaur plant eater to show the group is *Diplodocus.* It had a small head that held blunt teeth for stripping leaves and twigs from branches. Pictures of skulls are also good to show the kids. Most

dinosaur books have at least a few skull diagrams.

After discussing plant eaters and meat eaters, pass out copies of page 22. Ask the kids which kind of food—plants or meat—each circle represents. Then have them look closely at each dinosaur skull and draw lines from the skulls to the food their owners ate. Afterward, discuss each dinosaur, using the information below:

- *Edmontosaurus* (also known as *Anatosaurus*)—one of the duck-billed dinosaurs. It had 1500 teeth arranged in rows in the back of its mouth. *Edmontosaurus* used its teeth as grindstones to chop and crush rough plant material such as conifer needles. The old teeth were constantly replaced by new ones as they wore down.
- *Stegosaurus*—a plated dinosaur that used its turtlelike, beaked mouth to chop soft vegetation, then chomped the food with the small, weak teeth in the back of its mouth. (See page 44.)
- *Apatosaurus*—a large sauropod with peglike teeth for stripping off twigs and leaves.
- *Coelophysis*—a small carnivore that used its sharp, serrated teeth for catching and tearing its prey.
- *Allosaurus*—like *Tyrannosaurus,* this huge meat eater had many sharp, curved teeth that were serrated like a steak knife. *Allosaurus* had huge jaws that opened very wide for swallowing huge chunks of meat.

While you are talking about the different kinds of dinosaurs and what they ate, have the group compare dinosaur diets with those of modern animals. Ask them how *Tyrannosaurus* is like a tiger. (Both have sharp teeth and strong jaws for eating meat.) What kinds of modern animals travel in herds like *Apatosaurus* and use their teeth for browsing on leaves? (giraffes, deer)

Scientists think that some dinosaurs were *omnivores* (which means they ate both meat and plants). Can your group think of some modern omnivores? (raccoons, pigs, and people, to name a few)

Copycat Page

Draw a circle around the things that don't belong with the dinosaurs.

Draw a line from each dinosaur skull to the kind of food its owner would have eaten.

Stegosaurus

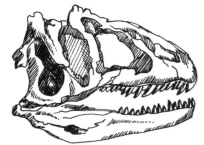

Allosaurus

Edmontosaurus

Coelophysis

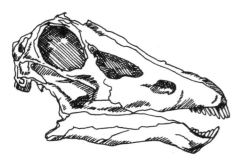

Apatosaurus

BEASTS, PAST AND PRESENT

Draw a line from the dinosaurs to the modern animals that they are like.

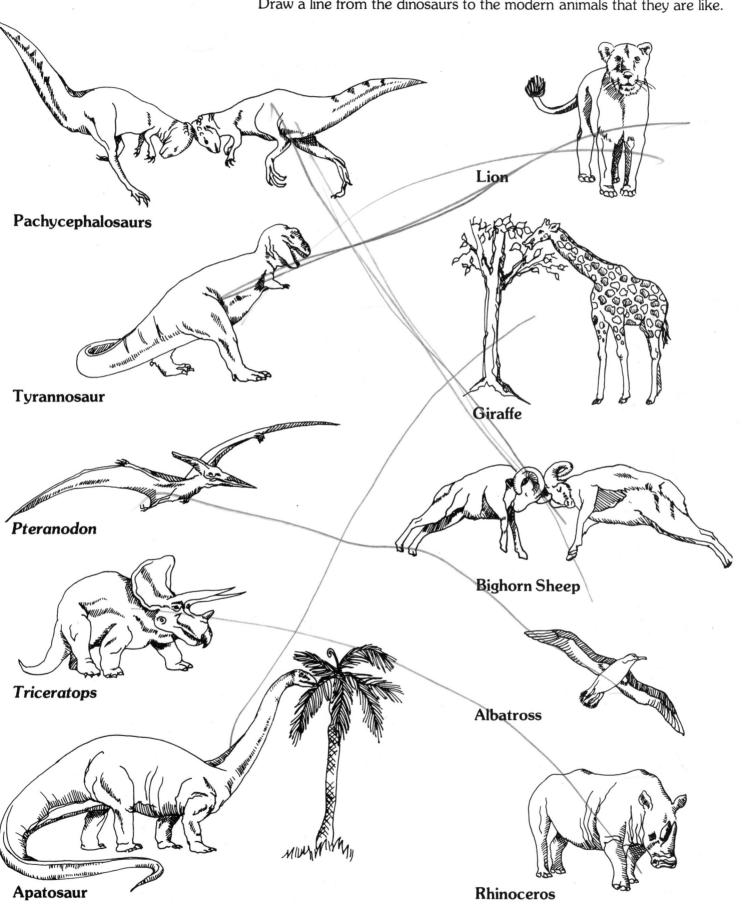

Pachycephalosaurs

Lion

Tyrannosaur

Giraffe

Pteranodon

Bighorn Sheep

Triceratops

Albatross

Apatosaur

Rhinoceros

WHEN THE DINOSAURS LIVED

N o one is sure exactly when life first appeared on earth. But fossils of simple life forms (bacteria) have been found in rocks that are over three *billion* years old.

Scientists have split the history of the earth into different stages called eras. The three most recent eras are the *Paleozoic Era* (the Age of Ancient Life), which began nearly 600 million years ago, the *Mesozoic Era* (the Age of Dinosaurs), which began about 245 million years ago, and the *Cenozoic Era* (the Age of Mammals), which began 65 million years ago. Each of these eras is further divided into time periods, based on major events that are recorded in the rocks.

The Paleozoic Era (600-245 million years ago)
"The Age of Ancient Life"

At the start of the Paleozoic Era, shallow seas covered most of the earth. Worms, jellyfish, trilobites, brachiopods, and seaweeds lived in the warm waters. Later in the Paleozoic the first fish appeared, followed by the first land-dwelling animals, the amphibians. Insects, reptiles, and land plants also made their first appearances. By the end of the Paleozoic coal was forming in lush swamps and tropical forests, and many reptiles had invaded the land.

The Mesozoic Era (245-65 million years ago)
"The Age of Dinosaurs"

At the start of the Mesozoic Era, all the continents that exist today were hooked together in a giant super-continent called *Pangaea*. In many places the climate was warm and humid, much as it is in the tropics today. The first mammals and the first dinosaurs appeared in the early part of the Mesozoic (during the *Triassic Period*). By the middle of the Mesozoic, during the *Jurassic Period*, Pangaea slowly began to break apart. The dinosaurs became huge and so did sea reptiles, flying reptiles, and even many plants. Insects were everywhere. And small shrewlike mammals lived on the forest floor, along with lizards and salamanders.

The last part of the Mesozoic (the *Cretaceous Period*) brought more changes and different kinds of dinosaurs. The continents had pulled apart and had begun to look as they do today. Flowering plants, birds, and dinosaurs thrived. But by the end of the Cretaceous there were massive animal die-offs. And by the time the Cenozoic Era began not a single dinosaur, flying reptile, or sea serpent was left.

The Cenozoic Era (65 million years ago to the present)
"The Age of Mammals"

When the Cenozoic Era began about 65 million years ago, the continents looked much as they do today. Most areas were warm and humid and the Alps, Himalayas, and Pyrenees were pushed up.

About the only reptiles that survived from the Mesozoic were the crocodiles, lizards, snakes, and turtles. Fish were common in the rivers, lakes, and seas. And many new kinds of birds had evolved.

As the Cenozoic went on, mammals began to branch out. There were herds of plant-eating hooved mammals, and many catlike and doglike meat eaters appeared. At first, all of the mammals were small. But later they grew to enormous sizes and the first whales, elephants, rhinos, and giant ground sloths appeared.

Less than five million years ago—around the time that the first humans evolved—saber-toothed cats, dire wolves, camels, and early horses were common. Many of these animals were caught in treacherous tar pits and preserved. And many became extinct only after the last Ice Age.

Many of the animals and plants survived the cold Ice Age temperatures, and their descendants are living today.

The Clock of Time

Scientists think the earth is about 4.6 billion years old. If you take this huge time span and compare it to a 24-hour clock, here's how life fits into the hours of the day and night:

The first living things would appear in the sea about eight o'clock in the morning.

The beginning of the *Paleozoic Era* (the Age of Ancient Life) wouldn't start until a little before nine o'clock at night.

Just before 11 PM, the Mesozoic Era (the Age of Dinosaurs) would begin. Then at a little past 11:30 the Cenozoic Era (the Age of Mammals) would begin.

Sometime after 11:59 and before midnight (less than a minute on this clock) the first human beings would appear. And all of human evolution and growth of civilization up to the present would occur in less than the remaining 30 seconds.

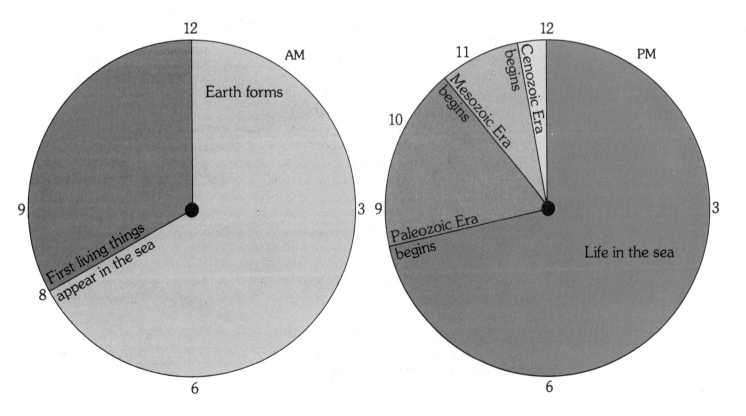

Annie Apatosaurus

Listen to a dinosaur story and act out the movements that go with it.

Objectives:
Describe a dinosaur that lived in the Mesozoic Era. Compare life today with life in the Mesozoic.

Ages:
Primary

Materials:
- *"Read-to-Me" story provided below*
- *pictures of Apatosaurus, Camptosaurus, Allosaurus, a pterosaur, and some scenes from the Mesozoic*

Subject:
Science

Sit in a circle with your group and ask if anyone knows what a dinosaur was. After each person has a chance to describe what he or she thinks these creatures were, explain that you are going to tell them a story about a special dinosaur named Annie. Annie was an *Apatosaurus.* Have everyone try to say the word "*Apatosaurus.*" Show the group a picture of an *Apatosaurus* or other large sauropod. (*Apatosaurus* used to be called *Brontosaurus.* But its name has been changed to *Apatosaurus* because this was the name first used to describe this dinosaur.) Now explain that *Apatosaurus* was a very large and heavy creature that walked slowly. Have the group imitate the sound of an *Apatosaurus* walking by slowing slapping their legs above their knees.

Next show them a picture of a *Camptosaurus.* Explain that *Camptosaurus* had very strong legs and could probably run very fast. Its speed helped *Camptosaurus* run away from hungry enemies.

Now show the kids a picture of a pterosaur. Explain that these creatures were not dinosaurs, but ancient reptiles that glided in the air and caught fish from lakes and shallow seas. Have the children stretch their arms out to the side to glide like pterosaurs.

Finally show the group a picture of an *Allosaurus.* Ask the children what they think it ate. Tell the kids that *Allosaurus* was a *predator,* just as hawks, owls, bobcats, and lions are today. It ate other animals. Have each person growl as *Allosaurus* might have growled.

Now read the following short story out loud, having the children "act out" the different dinosaurs. As you read, point to a picture of the dinosaur you are talking about. (Even though you have practiced, you'll probably have to remind them which movements and sounds go with each creature.)

ANNIE APATOSAURUS

A long, long, long time ago, in the Age of the Great Dinosaurs, there lived a huge dinosaur named Annie Apatosaurus. Annie was as long as two school buses parked end to end. And she weighed as much as five elephants! And every time Annie walked, the ground shook with her weight. (Have all the children slap their thighs very slowly to imitate Annie's walk.)

During the Age of the Great Dinosaurs, the weather was very warm and wet in many places—just as in the jungle today. There were huge trees and ferns everywhere. And lots of strange-looking creatures.

One day, Annie wandered away from her family. She was thirsty and wanted a drink at the lake. She walked and walked (have them continue to slap their thighs) until she came to the cool water. *Ahh* . . . she ducked her head in and took a big slurp. (Have the kids slurp.)

In the distance Annie could see five camptosaurs feeding on plants. (Ask the kids how many fingers five is.) The camptosaurs chomped their food slowly. *Chomp, chomp, chomp.* (Have the kids chomp.)

Suddenly, the camptosaurs stopped eating and looked up. Then they started to run as fast as they could! Soon Annie saw why they were running. They were being chased by a huge, hungry *Allosaurus.* Annie heard the *Allosaurus* growl as it ran. (Have everyone say *Allosaurus* and then growl as an *Allosaurus* might have growled.) Annie could see its long, long sharp teeth. And she heard it growl loudly again. (Have the kids growl again.) Annie decided she had better try to get away. So she turned and walked up a hill, far away from the hungry *Allosaurus.* (Have the kids slap their thighs.)

She walked a long way and came to another lake. She leaned over with her long neck and she slurped up another big drink. (Have everyone slurp.)

A huge pterosaur was soaring over her head. (Have the kids hold their arms out and "soar.") It swooped down to catch a fish, but missed and fell smack in the water with a big splash!

Annie clomped off to find something to eat. (Slap thighs.) In the distance she saw a clump of trees. When she got to the trees she stood up on her hind legs and stretched her neck up to snip off a tender twig from the top of a tree. She swallowed the twig whole, leaves and all. *Gulp!* Annie reached up for another twig, then another. She ate and ate until she was full.

Now Annie was getting tired and she knew it was time to find her family. Soon it would be dark. So she clomped back to the lake. (Slap thighs.) And there she saw her family getting a last drink for the evening. Annie took a last drink too (have kids slurp) and joined them as they all clomped off to find a place to spend the night. (Slap thighs.)

Soon they came to a nice, quiet spot. Then Annie and the rest of the apatosaurs all went to sleep. (Have the kids lay their heads on their hands.)

Ancient Days Travel Agent

Make a travel poster and brochure describing a trip to the Age of Dinosaurs.

Objective:
Describe a geologic time period within the Mesozoic Era (*the Age of Dinosaurs*).

Ages:
Primary and Intermediate

Materials:
- *poster board*
- *crayons, paint, or markers*
- *construction or drawing paper*
- *resources and reference books on the Age of Dinosaurs*
- *travel posters and brochures (optional)*

Subjects:
Science and Creative Writing

The Mesozoic Era (the Age of Dinosaurs) lasted 180 million years. During this time the super-continent *Pangea* broke apart, the first birds evolved, and flowering plants came to cover the land. Wouldn't it be exciting to be able to travel back in time millions of years to see what life was like during the Age of Dinosaurs?

Have your students become travel agents for the "Ancient Days Travel Company" and plan a tour to the era of the dinosaurs. (You can have your group work in teams or individually.)

Explain that the Mesozoic Era is divided into three periods: the Triassic, Jurassic, and Cretaceous. Each of these periods had its own geologic happenings, animals, plants, and types of dinosaurs.

Have each student choose one of these periods and then design a travel poster advertising that time period. Also have them write travel brochures giving the itinerary of the tour and what the time-traveling tourists might be able to see. (They'll need plenty of research time.) Tell them that travel companies work hard to entice travelers to choose their trips—so have them make their tours sound exciting. ("Visit the Jurassic. . . . See huge dinosaurs as they lumber through the plains and lush forests of prehistoric North America. . . .") Each brochure should also include details about how much the trip will cost and what visitors should bring along.

Bring in sample travel brochures and posters so your group can see what real ones look like. (Call a local travel agency to see if you can get some free samples.)

The children can create as many "fantasy" touches as they want—such as "Travel back in our new 707 time machine, equipped with . . . " But the actual descriptions of what each geologic time period was like—its climates and the animals and plants of the time—should be as realistic as possible.

The Span of Time

Make a human time line to demonstrate where the Age of Dinosaurs and other events fit into earth's history.

Objective:
Demonstrate the enormous amounts of time between major events in earth history by making a time line to scale.

Ages:
Intermediate and Advanced

Materials:
Outdoor Time Line-
- *yardstick*
- *masking tape*
- *balls of twine to equal 240 yards (216 m)*

Indoor Time Line-
- *ruler*
- *adding machine tape*
- *colored pencils or markers*
- *construction or drawing paper*
- *copies of page 30*

Subjects:
Science and Social Studies

I t's easy to say that the first life on earth appeared over three billion years ago. Or that the first dinosaur stomped along two hundred million years ago. But it's hard to comprehend just how much time a billion or a million years really is. In this activity your group can create a living picture of time by making a human time line.

Here are three analogies you can use to introduce the activity and to help your kids get a feel for the big numbers they'll be dealing with:

- It would take about three million kids, standing on top of each other's shoulders, to reach from the earth to the moon.

- If a person could live for a million days, he or she would be 2740 years old.

- In a billion seconds from 1989 it will be the year 2022.

Go on to explain that scientists estimate the earth's age to be nearly 4.6 *billion* years, or 4600 *million* years. Humans have been around for only a fraction of that time: about five million years. And about 60 million years before the first people walked the earth, the last dinosaurs stomped into extinction.

MAKING AN OUTDOOR TIME LINE

Find a space about 240 yards (216 m) long (about 2½ times the length of a football field). You will also need enough twine to stretch 240 yards, and some masking tape. (You will probably have to tie several balls of twine together.)

Mark off the twine in yards, using a yardstick and masking tape. (Cut off a piece of tape and attach it at every yard mark.)

Assign each person an event from the list on page 30. (Review the events with your kids and add more events if needed. The scale for the outdoor time line is ½ inch to every 250,000 years. If this is too large, use the smaller indoor scale shown in the first column on page 30 or make up your own scale to fit the space that's available.)

Have the person who represents the beginning of earth go all the way to one end

of the twine. Then have the rest of the students pace off the distance to their assigned events. For example, the person who represents the first algae would pace off 158 yards (142 m) from the present and the person who represents the first amphibian would pace off 18 yards (16 m).

Once the time line is complete, start with the origin of the earth and have the students call out what they are and how long ago they happened. (The person at the beginning of the earth will have to yell pretty loud.)

No matter which scale you use, you will not be able to fit in the events of modern time. All the "recent" students will be in a cluster at the end of the time line. The existence of people and all of human civilization is just a tiny fraction of the whole time line.

You can also do this activity inside, using the smaller scale listed on page 30. You can make the time line by plotting the events on a long strip of adding machine paper. Measure off the distances with a ruler. Explain to the kids that the length of the tape equals the age of the earth. Then assign an event to each child and have the kids draw pictures of their events. Tape the time line and pictures onto the wall. Since the modern events will all be crowded at the end, you can have the kids make a separate time line of recent history using a bigger scale. Attach the "recent" times below the longer time line, indicating that a lot has happened in only a short amount of time, compared to the age of the earth.

It's About Time

Make a time wheel of the history of life on earth.

Objectives:
Name the three eras that the history of life on earth is divided into. Give examples of the life forms that lived in each era.

Ages:
Intermediate and Advanced

Materials:
- copies of pages 31, 32, and 33
- scissors
- lightweight cardboard
- glue
- paper fasteners

Subject:
Science

Paleozoic, Mesozoic, Cenozoic—it's hard to keep geologic eras straight, especially when the time spans involved are so huge. By making a time wheel of the history of life on earth, your kids can see where everything fits in—from trilobites to the first fish, the coal swamps to the dinosaurs, and the first birds to the emergence of people.

Before starting on the wheel, explain that the history of life on earth is divided into three main eras: the Paleozoic (the Age of Ancient Life), the Mesozoic (the Age of Dinosaurs), and the Cenozoic (the Age of Mammals). (Scientists think that algae and some other simple life forms were living millions of years before the beginning of the Paleozoic, in the Precambrian. But these simple life forms didn't leave many fossils for paleontologists to study.)

Briefly discuss each of the three eras, explaining what the world was like during each one and the characteristic animals and plants of each. (See the background on page 24.)

To give the kids something to refer to as they make their wheels, you may want to list each era and its characteristics on the board.

Now give each child one copy each of pages 31, 32, and 33 (sheets A, B, and C). Also pass out two pieces of lightweight cardboard and a paper fastener to each person. Here's how to make the wheel:
1) Cut out the circles on sheets A and C and glue them to separate pieces of cardboard. Cut the excess cardboard from around both circles.
2) On the smaller circle, cut out the wedge to form a window. (Use pointed scissors.)
3) Poke a hole in the center of each circle with a sharp pencil or pen.
4) Cut out the wedges on sheet B. Explain that each of the wedges belongs in one of the three eras on the larger circle. There are three wedges per era.
5) Glue the wedges to the larger circle in the right eras. (The wedges do not represent specific time periods or the exact order of events.)
6) Finish the time wheel by attaching the smaller circle on top of the larger circle with a paper fastener.

Now have the kids divide into teams of two and quiz each other on what happened when.

(Indoor) Length from Present	(Outdoor) Length from Present	Years ago	Events
38 feet	254 yards	4.57 billion	Earth begins
29 feet	194 yards	3.5 billion	Life on earth begins
25 feet	167 yards	3 billion	First fossils form; algae, fungi, and bacteria are abundant
4.5 feet	31 yards	550 million	Jellyfish, sponges, and worms are abundant
3.75 feet	25 yards	450 million	First primitive fish
40 inches	22 yards	400 million	Earliest land plants (ferns and mosses)
35 inches	19 yards	350 million	Earliest land animals (amphibians)
31 inches	17 yards	310 million	First reptiles
27 inches	15 yards	270 million	Reptiles abundant and well developed
24.5 inches	14 yards	245 million	Age of Dinosaurs begins
18 inches	10 yards	180 million	Flowering plants develop
16 inches	9 yards	160 million	Birds evolve; dinosaurs abound
7 inches	4 yards	70 million	Modern birds develop
6 inches	11 feet	65 million	Dinosaurs extinct; Age of Mammals begins
5 inches	8 feet	50 million	Mammals and birds abundant
4 inches	7 feet	40 million	First elephants
.5 inch	10 inches	5 million	First humans
.15 inch	3 inches	1.5 million	Beginning of Pleistocene and Ice Ages
.001 inch	.02 inch	10,000	End of the most recent Ice Age
.0002 inch	.004 inch	1910	Mt. Vesuvius erupts in Pompeii
.0001 inch	.0015 inch	774	Magna Carta signed in 1215
.00002 inch	.0004 inch	213	Declaration of Independence signed in 1776

Scale   • Indoor: 1/10 inch = 1 million years   • Outdoor: 2 inches = 1 million years

Do you know what happened when? Glue the wedges on Sheet B to this circle in the right eras. Then attach the circle on Sheet C with a paper fastener. You've got your own Time Wheel!

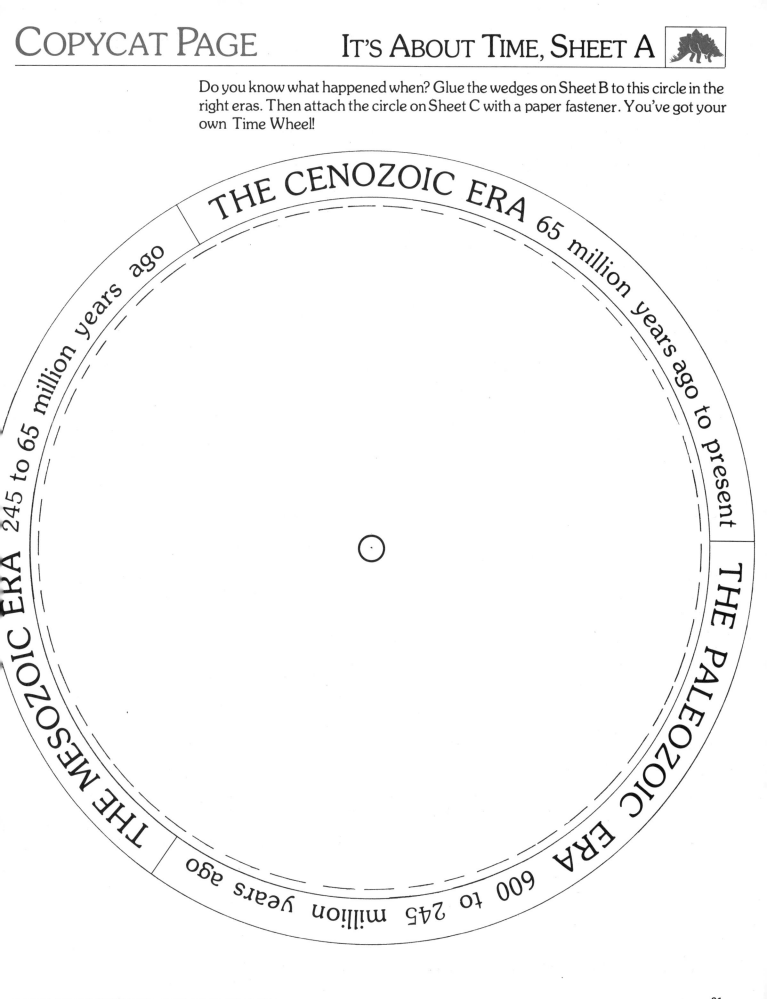

THE CENOZOIC ERA 65 million years ago to present

THE PALEOZOIC ERA 600 to 245 million years ago

THE MESOZOIC ERA 245 to 65 million years ago

The Great Lakes were formed

The Grand Canyon was shaped

Dinosaurs were abundant

Coral reefs flourished

Insects and amphibians developed

Fish developed

Diatryma, a seven-foot tall meat-eating bird, roamed the plains.

Huge rhinoceroses and three-toed horses roamed

Trilobites thrived

Brachiopods were common

Land plants began to develop

Pterosaurs appeared

Cycads and conifers developed

Reptiles developed

Coal swamps appeared

Mammals and birds appeared

Flowering plants emerged

People roamed the planet

The Ice Ages occurred

Mammoths and saber-toothed cats thrived

On this time wheel are the three most recent eras that the history of life on earth is divided into. The first era is the Paleozoic, or the Age of Ancient Life. All animal life was in the sea at the beginning of this time. But by the end of the Paleozoic, amphibians and reptiles were crawling through the warm, lush forests. Other reptiles were gliding through the sky. And huge insects were flying all around.

The middle era is the Mesozoic, or the Age of Dinosaurs. Mammals and birds developed during this time, but the dinosaurs "ruled" the planet.

The dinosaurs had disappeared by the time the Cenozoic, or the Age of Mammals, started. The earth went through several Ice Ages at the end of this era. Mammals—especially people—became the new "rulers" of the planet.

Clues From The Past

It's hard to imagine a herd of six-ton (5.5 t) *Triceratops* stampeding across what is now Montana. Or a 75-foot (22-m) *Brachiosaurus* laying eggs in the sand. But that's exactly the challenge that faces paleontologists—putting life into the dinosaurs and trying to imagine how they lived. And they do this by studying fossil clues.

How Paleontologists Dig Up Clues

Most paleontologists are trained as biologists and geologists. As geologists, they must piece together clues about rocks—how rocks form, how they change over time, and what environments they represent—in order to know which rock layers might contain dinosaur fossils. As biologists, they have to understand anatomy, physiology, ecology, and behavior in order to know how to read the fossil clues.

Many paleontologists work part of the year in the field—digging up fossils, covering them with huge protective plaster casts, and making notes on the geology of the area. Then they take their fossil finds back to the museum or university where they work. For the rest of the year they analyze the fossils they have found, write papers to explain their findings to other scientists, and teach or give lectures about prehistoric life.

What Are Fossils?

Fossils are the remains or evidence of ancient organisms preserved in rock or some other material, such as tar or permafrost. Everything that we know about dinosaurs originates with fossil clues.

How Fossils Form

Only a few of the millions of dinosaurs that lived became fossilized. That's because fossils are formed only under special conditions, and it's just chance that determines which animals die in the right places and which don't.

Once an animal dies, the soft parts of its body such as the skin, muscles, and internal organs rot away quickly. But the teeth, bones, and shells usually last longer, especially if they are buried in mud, sand, or silt. (Usually a plant or animal has to be buried before a fossil will form. Burying protects bones and shells from weather damage, rotting, and scavengers.)

Sometimes water will carry calcite, silica, iron, and other minerals to the pores and other spaces in a bone. Eventually these spaces fill with minerals and turn into stone, while the rest of the bone stays in its original form. Whole skeletons, including teeth, can become preserved in this way. *Fossil molds* can also form under special conditions. Water seeping into rocks will dissolve the bones of an animal and leave a hollow place in the ground. (The hollow is the same shape as the object.) This type of fossil is called a *mold*. If the mold fills in with minerals, the fossil that's formed is called a *cast*.

Many times footprints and skin impressions also become filled in with minerals or mud and become fossilized.

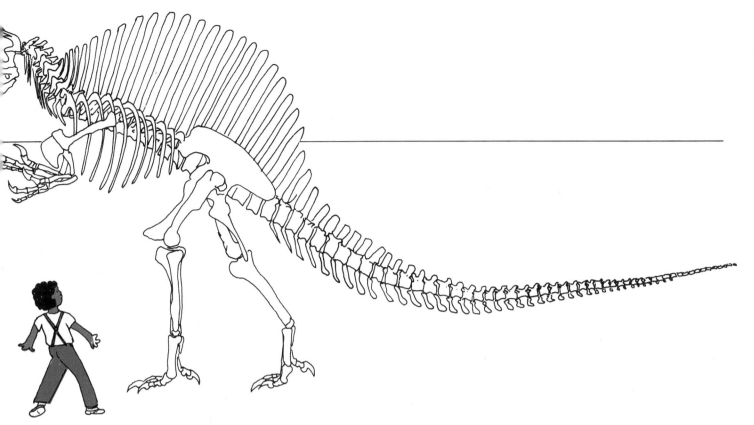

Fossilized dinosaur remains have been discovered only in rocks. But other prehistoric creatures have been preserved in sticky tar pits (saber-toothed cats, dire wolves, and other creatures), amber (insects and plants), and ice (woolly mammoths).

Fossils Push Up

Many fossils form at the bottoms of lakes and streams. Over a period of thousands of years, an animal's bones and teeth get covered with many layers of mud and sand. In time, these layers are compressed into rock or become cemented together by minerals, and the fossils get buried deeper in the ground.

But the inside of the earth is constantly moving and changing. Enormous pressures and heat build up, forcing continents to move and land to be uplifted.

When the land is uplifted, fossils buried deep in the ground may be pushed up near the surface. As the rocks covering the fossils are exposed, the fossils appear, sometimes after being buried for millions of years.

The Case of the Hole in the Head, the Vanishing Herds, the Midget Arms, and Other Dinosaur Mysteries

Why did the dinosaurs disappear 65 million years ago? Why did the 88-foot (26-m) *Diplodocus* have a hole in the top of its head? Why did so many of the duck-billed dinosaurs have such oddly shaped head crests? Why did *Tyrannosaurus* have such tiny front arms—too small to reach its jaws?

These are just a few of the dinosaur mysteries that are keeping paleontologists guessing. (See page 57 in the Appendix for more on dinosaur mysteries.) As in all scientific problems, though, paleontologists try to solve their mysteries one step at a time. First they observe and investigate all the evidence they can find. Then they try to come up with a *hypothesis* (possible answer) that might solve the mystery. Only when a hypothesis has been proven does it become *fact*.

Mapping the Dinosaurs

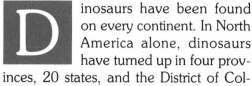

Make a poster showing where dinosaur fossils have been found.

Objective:
Point to countries, provinces and states where dinosaurs have been found.

Ages:
Primary and Intermediate

Materials:
- *copies of page 43*
- *copies of an outline map of the United States and Canada*
- *atlas*
- *yarn*
- *pushpins*
- *rulers*
- *construction paper*
- *glue*

Subjects:
Science and Geography

Dinosaurs have been found on every continent. In North America alone, dinosaurs have turned up in four provinces, 20 states, and the District of Columbia. To find out which dinosaurs have been found where in North America, try this mapping activity with your group.

Pass out copies of page 43. Also pass out copies of an 8½ × 11" outline map of the United States and Canada. (If possible, find a map that has the borders drawn in for the states and provinces but that doesn't have any names. If you don't have one, just make your own by tracing from an atlas.)

Next give each person a sheet of 12 × 18" construction paper. Have the kids paste their maps to the center of the construction paper. Then have them cut out the nine dinosaur squares and paste them all around the map in the margin on the construction paper.

Next have them draw a line (using a ruler) from each dinosaur to the state or province where it was discovered. (The places are listed on the pictures.)

BRANCHING OUT TO THE WORLD

To help children learn where different countries are, make a "World of Dinosaur Discoveries" bulletin board. Pin a large map of the world to the bulletin board, leaving a margin on all sides. Explain to your group how to use an atlas to find out where a country or state is located. Then have all the children draw their favorite dinosaurs on construction paper to paste around the world map as decorations.

Now write the names of each of the countries, states, and provinces listed below on a separate slip of paper and have each person come up, one at a time, and pick a name. (Explain beforehand that dinosaurs have been discovered in all these places.) Each person must find the place on the map, point to it with a pointer, and stick a pin on that location.

As a variation to this, you can paste up pictures of dinosaurs from around the world and then connect the dinosaur pictures to the places they were found, using yarn and pushpins. (To find out which dinosaurs have been found where, see the chart on page 60 in the Appendix or look in *The Illustrated Dinosaur Dictionary* by Helen Roney Sattler.)

Countries, States, and Provinces Where Dinosaurs Have Been Discovered:

Argentina, Australia, Belgium, Brazil, Canada (Alberta, British Columbia, Nova Scotia, Northwest Territories, Saskatchewan, Yukon), China, Egypt, England, France, Germany, Holland, Hungary, India, Israel, Japan, Madagascar, Mexico, Mongolia, Morocco, Niger, Portugal, Russia, Scotland, South Africa, Tanzania, Uruguay, Zimbabwe, United States (Alabama, Alaska, Arizona, Arkansas, Colorado, Connecticut, District of Columbia, Kansas, Maryland, Massachusetts, Michigan, Mississippi, Missouri, Montana, New Jersey, New Mexico, North Carolina, Oklahoma, South Dakota, Texas, Utah, Wyoming)

Clue Finders

"Solve" a dinosaur mystery and use clues to figure out modern animal mysteries.

Objectives:
Explain how paleontologists use clues to solve dinosaur mysteries. Use clues to solve simple animal mysteries.

Ages:
Primary, Intermediate, and Advanced

Materials:
* *copies of page 44*
* *magazine pictures*
* *large envelopes*
* *paper and pencils*
* *animal clues*

Subject:
Science

I magine how frustrating it is sometimes to be a paleontologist. You study things that lived millions of years ago, but you can never travel back in time to see what they were really like. Instead, your only clues are bones, teeth, and tracks in the rock. You have to use this evidence to reconstruct a picture of life in the past.

In the first part of this activity, your group will get a chance to learn how paleontologists have tried to solve a real dinosaur mystery. In the second part, your group will become modern-day scientists and try to solve animal mysteries using clue packets.

PART I: DINOSAUR DETECTIVES

The mystery below describes how paleontologists have tried to piece together clues to figure out why *Stegosaurus* had bony plates on its back. Go through the story with your group and talk about how the scientists proposed possible solutions (hypotheses) and then had to rethink their "guesses" as new clues turned up. As you go along, see if the children can make some guesses. (Even though it's difficult, they will get an idea of how scientists try to put clues together.)

THE MYSTERY OF THE PLATES ON THE BACK

Read this to the group: Over 100 years ago, a group of paleontologists dug up a complete skeleton of a large dinosaur, now known as *Stegosaurus*. Measuring the skeleton from its nose to its tail, they found that it was about 30 feet (9 m) long. The bones of the hind legs measured about twice as long as the bones of the front legs, and there were four bony spikes lying near the end of the tail.

Mixed in with the skeleton were 20 very strange-looking bones. These bones were flat and shaped sort of like triangles. Some of them were more than 20 inches (50 cm) long.

Now pass out page 44. Once everyone has a copy, continue reading:

The paleontologists wanted to figure out several things about this skeleton. First, how did the plates fit on the dinosaur's body? And second, what was the purpose of these strange, triangular bones?

Since that first discovery, scientists have made some educated guesses about the plates, using what's been pieced together about how the animal lived. By looking at the skull, for example, it was clear to scientists that *Stegosaurus* was a plant eater. (Have the group look at picture 1. Ask them if they know why the scientists decided *Stegosaurus* ate plants. Then ask if anyone has any guesses at this point about how *Stegosaurus* used its plates.)

Now read on: Since plant-eating animals are usually food for meat eaters, it seemed likely that *Stegosaurus* was hunted by meat-eating dinosaurs. That meant that it needed some way to protect itself from hungry enemies. Running away probably wasn't the answer. *Stegosaurus's* front legs were so short and its head so close to the ground that a quick getaway probably would have been pretty difficult. So the scientists reasoned that maybe *Stegosaurus* was protected by its odd spikes and plates. Since the spikes were found lying near the end of the tail, it made sense that they would have been attached to the tail on a living *Stegosaurus*. In this position the spikes could do a lot of damage to an attacker when the tail swung back and forth.

But what about the plates? It seemed that the only place they could have fit was along the dinosaur's back. Some scientists suggested that, in this position, the plates may have served as a kind of armor. But

(continued next page)

other scientists weren't so sure that this was the plates' main purpose. (Ask the kids if they can say why, then read on.) True, they could have protected Stegosaurus's backbone. But wouldn't a meat eater still have been able to attack the dinosaur's tender sides and belly?

Then another scientist made an educated guess about the plates. Maybe Stegosaurus used them to "advertise" for a mate. After all, a lot of modern animals have special features that help them attract the opposite sex. (Have the kids look at picture 2. Then ask them if they can think of some of the features that help modern animals attract mates. Examples include antlers, the showy feathers of male peacocks, and the colorful throat patches of some lizards.)

But many scientists felt that, while attracting a mate may have been part of the purpose for Stegosaurus's plates, it probably wasn't their main purpose any more than protection from enemies was. The plates seemed way too big and bulky to carry around just to attract a mate.

Paleontologists then came up with another idea. They had noticed that each plate was covered with a lot of grooves. And inside each plate was a mass of spongy bone. This spongy bone was full of tunnels that branched out in many directions.

The scientists decided that the grooves on the plates and the tunnels inside the plates may have held blood vessels. And they already knew that Stegosaurus was a reptile like all other dinosaurs, which meant that it was probably cold-blooded. Being a cold-blooded animal meant that on a cool day Stegosaurus's blood was also cool, and so was Stegosaurus itself. But the heat of a warm day would warm up Stegosaurus's blood, raising the dinosaur's body temperature too.

With all of these ideas in mind, the scientists came up with a new hypothesis: Maybe Stegosaurus used its plates to help it cool off or warm up. (Have the kids look at picture 3.) On a hot day it could pump blood into the vessels and tunnels of its plates. The vessels on the plates were probably right under the skin. So when a breeze blew across the plates, it could cool the blood in the vessels and in that way help keep Stegosaurus cool.

The scientists figured that, on a cold day, Stegosaurus could shut off most of the blood supply to the plates. That way it could conserve its body heat when it needed to.

Scientists aren't yet sure if this latest explanation of the plates as "cooling and warming mechanisms" is the answer. Since they can't observe a living Stegosaurus, it's very difficult to prove why this strange dinosaur carried plates on its back. But scientists are still working on this and on many other dinosaur mysteries. (For information about other dinosaur mysteries, see page 57 in the Appendix.)

PART 2: ANIMAL SCRAMBLE

Now that you've introduced dinosaur mysteries, turn your group into modern-day paleontologists to see if they can solve some twentieth-century animal mysteries. In this activity they will try to use picture clues to guess a mystery creature. It should help them understand how a scientist uses clues to make inferences about something unknown.

First divide the group into teams of three or four children. Give each team a numbered packet (a large envelope works well) that contains clues about a specific animal. None of the clues should give the animal away, but all of the clues together should point to it. (You can write out clues, draw symbols and scenes, or cut out pictures from magazines.) Here are some examples:

Crocodile or Alligator
- picture of shoes and a purse with scales
- picture of a swamp
- picture of eggs
- picture of a turtle, snake, or dinosaur that says "my relative"

Tiger
- box of Frosted Flakes
- map of India
- piece of material with stripes
- picture of a house cat

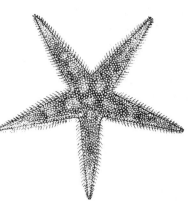

Turkey
- a feather
- bones from a chicken or turkey
- an advertisement for stuffing
- picture of a Pilgrim

Butterfly
- picture of flowers
- picture of a herd of migrating animals
- picture of a butterfly net
- six legs circled on picture of people or animals

Goat
- piece of a milk carton
- the name "Heidi"
- a tin can
- the word "billy"

Elephant
- picture of a piano keyboard
- picture of a circus
- picture of the African savannah
- handful of peanuts

Starfish
- the number 5 written down
- picture of a beach
- picture of the sun or a constellation
- picture of a fish

Mouse
- picture of a Christmas tree
- calendar with December 24th circled
- picture of Swiss cheese
- picture of scientists in white lab coats
- picture of a hawk, owl, or some other animal that eats mice

Have the students work in groups to decide which animals the clues point to. Then have them write their guesses down and pass the packet on to another group.

After everyone has seen all the envelopes, discuss each set of clues and how each clue relates to the animals. Then tie in the idea of using clues with paleontology.

Tracking the Dinosaurs

Make a potato print mural of dinosaur tracks.

Objective:
Describe how fossilized dinosaur tracks formed. Simulate a fossil story from the past.

Ages:
Intermediate and Advanced

Materials:
- *brown butcher paper or grocery bags*
- *potatoes (at least one per two students)*
- *clay-carving tools or paper clips*
- *tempera paint*
- *flat pan for paint*
- *markers*

Subjects:
Science and Art

A dinosaur runs through the mud along a stream, leaving a trail of tracks as it goes. Over time, new layers of mud cover the tracks. As more time goes by, layer after layer covers the dinosaur tracks. The covering of mud gets heavier, pressing down on the tracks. Slowly the tracks change into rock.

Paleontologists can learn a lot from fossilized dinosaur tracks. They can tell, for example, whether a dinosaur was walking, running, or even swimming by how far apart its tracks are, how the tracks are lined up, and how far each foot pressed down into the mud. Scientists can also tell if a dinosaur was traveling by itself or with others, whether the tracks were made by adults or young, and how big the track makers were. And, by studying the types of prints and the changes in direction that they take, scientists have been able to see where one dinosaur was chasing another.

Have the children think about the tracks they would leave while walking or running in wet soil or sand. Ask them how the tracks of their parents would be different from theirs. How would a dog's tracks look different from a person's? From a bird's?

Now have the group create their own dinosaur tracks on butcher paper or large brown grocery bags, using potato printers (see following page). The potatoes will be the dinosaurs' feet and the paper will be the soft mud where the tracks were made.

(continued next page)

MAKING POTATO PRINTS

To make a dinosaur foot, cut a potato in half lengthwise. (You can do this ahead of time, but keep the potatoes in cold water until the kids are ready to use them.)

Dry the flat surface of the potato and draw the outline of a dinosaur's foot with a marker. (See examples below.) Carve away the potato around the foot, using clay tools or a paper clip. The "foot" should stick up about 1/4 inch (6 mm).

To make a stream bank mural, take a long sheet of butcher paper and have all the students work together to create trails of tracks and tales of caught prey or battles and escapes. The "feet" can be pressed gently into a thin layer of tempera paint and then printed onto the paper.

Your group can also create dinosaur track stationery and note cards to send to their friends.

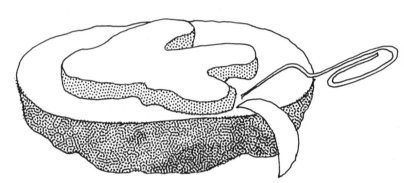

The Tooth, Claw, and Bone Mystery Hunt

Make "fossils" and use math to discover where they've been buried.

Objectives:
Explain and demonstrate how a fossil forms. Estimate distances using dinosaur measurements. Compare dinosaur sizes.

Ages:
Intermediate and Advanced

Materials:
- *aluminum foil pans of various sizes (or ½ gallon milk cartons)*
- *plaster of Paris*
- *gravel or sand*
- *crushed or powdered charcoal or powdered tempera paints (optional)*
- *copies of page 42*
- *shells, bones, teeth, or other hard objects (supplied by the children)*
- *rulers or yardsticks—one for each team*

(continued next page)

T racking down fossils can be exciting. Imagine digging up a nine-foot (2.7-m) shoulder blade of an *Ultrasaurus*. Or a six-inch (15-cm) tooth of a *Tyrannosaurus*. In this activity, your group will get a chance to track down mystery fossils using special "dinosaur" clues. The first day the kids make their own fossils and the second day they go on the mystery hunt. Here's how to do it:

MAKING MYSTERY FOSSILS

Before the hunt begins, have each person make a mystery fossil. You can also divide the kids into teams and have each team work together to make a fossil. Each of the teams will need foil pans or milk cartons, plaster of Paris, sand or fine gravel, water, a bowl or small bucket of water (for rinsing plaster from hands before it sets), and something to fossilize, such as a jawbone, tooth, chicken bone, or shell. (If you use chicken bones, boil them beforehand to get all the meat off.) To make the fossils, have each team follow these steps:

1) Clean off the objects to be buried and cover them with a thin coating of petroleum jelly.

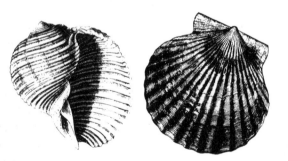

2) Mix the dry ingredients in these proportions: one part gravel or sand to one part plaster of Paris. (As an option, you can add one part crushed charcoal or powdered tempera to color the plaster so that it looks more rocklike.)

3) When the dry ingredients are thoroughly

40

- *several balls of twine or yarn*
- *paper and pencils*
- *masking tape*
- *petroleum jelly*
- *several bowls or small buckets*

Subjects:
Science and Math

PLASTER

SHELLS, BONES, OR OTHER OBJECTS

PLASTER

SAND

PETROLEUM JELLY

mixed, add just enough water to make the mixture pasty. (Be extra careful—too much water will keep the mixture from drying completely.) Coat the bottom and sides of the foil pan or milk carton with a little petroleum jelly, then sprinkle in a little sand or dirt. Next pour about half of the plaster mixture into the pan. Have someone continuously stir the plaster that's still in the bucket. (This will keep it from setting up too soon.)

4) Lay the cleaned objects randomly in the plaster. (Don't mix different kinds of items in one container. For example, use all shells or all bones to make each fossil.)

5) Then pour the rest of the plaster into the foil pan (or milk carton) to cover the objects. Let all the mystery fossils dry thoroughly. It will take up to 24 hours.

6) Remove the fossils from the containers.

SETTING UP THE TRAIL

Now that the fossils are made, you need to set up the hunt. Pick four of the fossils (or one for each team) to hide. Use a large playground, a field, or another open spot for the hunt. Each team will be starting off from a different spot, but will be going the same number of feet.

We've made a sample set of clues for a 100-foot (30-m) trail. (See page 42.) You can easily adjust it to make the hunt longer or shorter. (To make adjustments, just use the measurements listed on page 42.) You can also rearrange the clues for each group so that no one has exactly the same set.

Make four 150-foot (43-m) lines with yarn or twine, from four different spots around the school or nature center. At the 100-foot (30-m) mark, bury one of the fossils, leaving a little bit exposed as a clue.

THE HUNT IS ON

On the day of the hunt, pass out a copy of page 42 to each team. Also pass out a yardstick, paper and pencils, and masking tape. Explain that each team must figure out the math clues to find a special mystery fossil that is hidden somewhere along the line. For example, the first clue might say *"Go the length of 18 Triceratops brow horns."* On the measurement list it says that one brow horn is equal to 40 inches (100 cm). The team members must first figure out the length of 18 brow horns and then measure off that distance on their trail. For those children who may "run ahead" to find their fossils, you can set up a few "dummy holes" to stress the importance of accurate measurements.

Once each team finds the plaster rock containing the hidden fossil, they must dig it up and take it to the "fossil cleaning station." Have old toothbrushes, blunt knives, and carving tools there so that they can carefully remove the plaster covering from their fossil to find out what they have.

While the kids are working, stress the importance of being careful not to break the fragile fossils. The team that is the first to thoroughly clean their fossil wins the hunt. (Before you leave the area, make sure all the holes are filled in and it looks as it did before the hunt.)

THE MEASUREMENTS

DINOSAUR	PART	MEASUREMENT
Psittacosaurus	Babies	10 in. (25 cm)
Triceratops	Brow Horn	40 in. (100 cm)
Diplodocus	Brain	4 in. (10 cm)
Allosaurus	Footprint	1 ft. (30 cm)
Ultrasaurus	Shoulder Blade	9 ft. (2.7 m)
Tyrannosaurus	Tooth	6 in. (15 cm)
Pteranodon	Wingspan	26 ft. (7.8 m)
Spinosaurus	Spine	2 yd. (1.8 m)
Tyrannosaurus	Skull	4 ft. (1.2 m)
Pachycephalosaurus	Whole body length	15 ft. (4.5 m)
Brachiosaurus	Whole body length	75 ft. (22.5 m)
Stegosaurus	Plates	30 in. (75 cm)

THE CLUES: HOW TO FIND YOUR BURIED FOSSIL

1. Go the length of 6 *Psittacosaurus babies*.
2. Go the length of 1 *Pachycephalosaurus*.
3. Go the length of 1 *Diplodocus brain*.
4. Go 1/10 the length of 1 *Brachiosaurus*.
5. Go the length of 1 *Pteranodon wingspan*.
6. Go the length of 5 *Allosaurus footprints*.
7. Go the length of 4 *Triceratops brow horns*.
8. Go the length of 5 *Stegosaurus plates*.
9. Go the length of 1 *Spinosaurus spine*.
10. Go the length of 1 *Psittacosaurus baby*.
11. Go the length of 7 *Tyrannosaurus teeth*.
12. Go 1/2 the length of a *Tyrannosaurus skull*.
13. Go 1/3 the length of an Ultrasaurus *shoulder blade*.

Corythosaurus
(ko-RITH-uh-SAWR-us)
Alberta

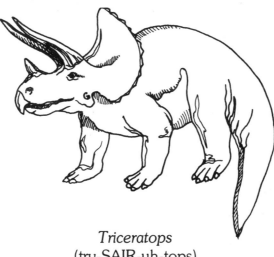

Triceratops
(try-SAIR-uh-tops)
Alberta, Montana, Saskatchewan,
Wyoming, North and South Dakota

Coelophysis
(see-lo-FISE-iss)
Arizona, New Mexico, Texas

Ammosaurus
(AM-uh-SAWR-us)
rizona, Massachusetts, Nova Scotia

Acrocanthosaurus
(ak-ro-KANTH-uh- SAWR-us)
Oklahoma

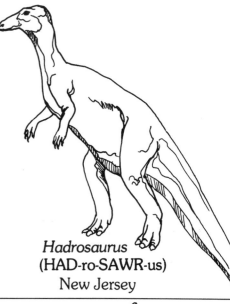

Hadrosaurus
(HAD-ro-SAWR-us)
New Jersey

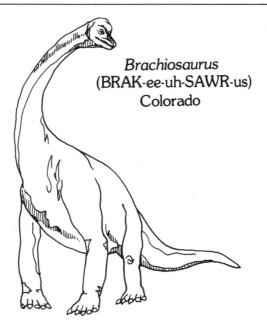

Brachiosaurus
(BRAK-ee-uh-SAWR-us)
Colorado

Nodosaurus
(no-doe-SAWR-us)
Wyoming

Stegosaurus
(STEG-uh-SAWR-us)
Utah, Colorado

43

STEGOSAURUS WAS A PLANT EATER

1

STEGOSAURUS
SKULL

2

DID *STEGOSAURUS* USE ITS PLATES TO ATTRACT A MATE?

3

"THE PLATES ON THE BACK MYSTERY" IS SOLVED! (MAYBE!)

A CREATIVE LOOK AT DINOSAURS

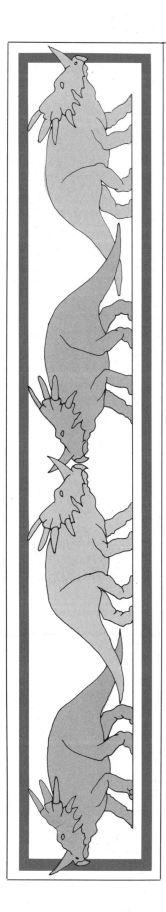

Everywhere you look there are dinosaurs—on T-shirts, in museums, on TV, in cartoon strips, in books, on cereal boxes, in advertisements, in toy stores, and even in the movies. For animals that have been extinct for over 65 million years, that's quite a feat!

But it's no wonder—huge beasts covered with horns, spikes, and frills can really stimulate imaginations. Here are some of the creative ways dinosaurs have lumbered into our lives:

Dinosaurs in Print

In the early 1900s dinosaurs became a big literary hit. Jules Verne's *Journey to the Center of the Earth* and Sir Arthur Conan Doyle's *The Lost World* were filled with accounts of dinosaurs and other prehistoric creatures living in the modern world. Tarzan creator Edgar Rice Burroughs also used the intrigue of dinosaurs in his popular novels. Tarzan's prehistoric adventures were a big success in comic book form too—and they also made their way into syndicated comic strips in newspapers.

Dinosaurs on the Screen

Dinosaurs and other prehistoric life have intrigued movie producers as well as authors. People flocked to the screen to see "The Lost World," "One Million Years B.C.," "King Kong," and over a dozen Godzilla flicks. And once they'd invaded the movies, it was only a matter of time before dinosaurs and other prehistoric animals made it onto the TV screen. Cartoon dinosaurs appear in "The Flintstones," the well-known cartoon series about "modern" Stone Age people. The time periods in the Flintstones are a little mixed up—dinosaurs were long gone by the time people evolved—but it's still fun to watch Fred, Barney, and the others operating *Brontosaurus* cranes and flying on pterodactyl airplanes.

Dinosaurs in Art and Music

You probably don't have a painting of a hadrosaur hanging over your mantel or a figurine of a tyrannosaur sitting on your coffee table. But dinosaur art does exist, thanks to Charles Knight, William Stout, Sylvia Czerkas, and others. The late Charles Knight was one of the first artists to merge artistic ideas about how dinosaurs looked with scientific ideas about how they lived. More recently, William Stout has added a touch of fantasy to dinosaur art in his prehistoric paintings. And Sylvia Czerkas sculpts dinosaurs and other prehistoric animals in authentic detail.

Music is another cultural area that dinosaurs have "invaded." True, you aren't likely to hear many dinosaur songs on the radio. But there are albums that are chock-full of dinosaur music. One is *Dinosaur Rock* by Michele Valerie and Michael Stein. *Dinosaur Rock* tells a children's story through songs like "The Hadrosaur from Hackensack," "Stella Stegosaurus," "The Sauropod Swing," and nine other Mesozoic melodies. (For information on how to order, see page 63 in the Appendix.)

The activities in this section take a creative look at dinosaurs. We hope they will inspire some dinosaur creativity in your children!

Dinosaur Dancing

Move to music, the way different dinosaurs might have moved.

Objective:
Relate the size and structure of dinosaurs to how they moved.

Ages:
Primary

Materials:
- *pictures of dinosaurs*
- *music*
- *cymbals, wood blocks, and other rhythm instruments (optional)*

Subjects:
Science and Drama

Here's a way to get your kids out of their seats and into step with the dinosaurs. But before the dancing begins, show your group pictures of the dinosaurs they will be imitating. Talk a little about each dinosaur, explaining how it lived and how it might have moved. For example, as you hold up a picture of *Tyrannosaurus* (the "tyrant lizard"), tell the kids that this dinosaur was an aggressive meat eater. Scientists who have studied *Tyrannosaurus's* fossilized tracks think that this beast probably chased down its prey with long strides, placing one foot in line with the other. Its short arms were equipped with sharp claws for holding onto the animals it caught.

Here's a rundown of some other well-known dinosaurs the kids can imitate:

Apatosaurus ("deceptive lizard"), also known as *Brontosaurus* ("thunder lizard")—This beast was a giant, even among dinosaurs. From the tip of its nose to the end of its tail, *Apatosaurus* measured 70 feet (21 m)—longer than two school buses! It used its long, flexible neck to reach the leaves and twigs and evergreen needles on which it browsed. *Apatosaurus* didn't move very fast. Most likely it lumbered along at about four miles (6 km) per hour.

Edmontosaurus ("duck lizard")—This was one of the duck-billed dinosaurs. It used its ducklike "bill" to chop off twigs and other plant food. Some scientists think *Edmontosaurus* could swim, using its strong tail to help it move through the water.

Ornithomimus ("bird mimic")—This small, lightweight dinosaur had hollow bones. With its long, birdlike legs, it chased down lizards and small mammals for its meals. It also ate fruit and possibly the eggs of other dinosaurs.

Once you've talked about some of the different dinosaurs, get ready to hold a dance session. Clear a space for a dance floor, get the kids on their feet, and start the music. (If you have some non-dancers in your group, give them cymbals, wood blocks, tambourines, or other rhythm instruments so they can keep the beat.) For the *Brontosaurus* Boogie, try playing "In the Mood" or some other medium-paced swing music. Have the kids imitate *Apatosaurus* by raising their hands above their heads to form the dinosaur's long neck. One hand laid over the other can be the beast's head.

To dance the *Tyrannosaurus* Tromp, have the kids strut around the room as they curl their fingers into claws and hold their arms close to their bodies. The "Theme from Jaws" seems to fit the fearsome *Tyrannosaurus* perfectly.

The *Ornithomimus* Bird Bop will really burn off some excess energy. Bluegrass or some other fast-paced music suits the quick, birdlike movements of this dinosaur. The kids can pretend to chase lizards and other small animals.

The Dance of the *Edmontosaurus* is a relaxing way to wind down your dance session. Use graceful, flowing music—Tchaikovsky's "Swan Lake" or Pachelbel's "Canon in D," for example. Have the kids move slowly and calmly to "feed" on plants, placing one hand over the palm of the other to form the dinosaur's ducklike bill. You can also have them "swim" like an *Edmontosaurus*.

Bruce Norfleet

Tons of Trivia

Make a bulletin board of "fascinating prehistoric facts."

Objective:
List five dinosaur-related facts.

Ages:
Primary and Intermediate

Materials:
- *construction paper*
- *scissors*
- *felt-tipped markers*
- *copies of page 50 (optional)*

Subject:
Science

People everywhere are fascinated with trivia. Trivia pages are regular features in many magazines, and there are dozens of trivia books to read and games to play.

Some of the biggest trivia buffs are children. They love hearing about the fastest, the biggest, the oldest, the smallest, and so on. Have your group put their trivia curiosity to work on a "Fascinating Prehistoric Facts" bulletin board about dinosaurs, fossils, paleontologists, and other dinosaur-related subjects. You can either have the kids find their own facts or let them each pick one from the list on page 50. (If you want them to find their own facts, don't pass the list out until the children have finished researching.)

Once everyone has a bit of trivia, have each student cut a piece of construction paper into a shape that has something to do with his or her fact. Then have the kids print their facts on the shapes. For example, a fact about *Tyrannosaurus* could be written on a *Tyrannosaurus* silhouette. A dinosaur footprint could be the shape for a fact about the length of a dinosaur's stride. And the shape of a skull or bone would be perfect for a bit of fossil trivia.

To make your "Fascinating Prehistoric Facts" bulletin board, first line the board with construction paper. Cut out letters in the shape of bones for the title, then have the kids tack their facts all over the board.

Ancient Advertising

Use the dinosaur theme to create advertisements.

Objective:
Create an advertisement using dinosaurs.

Ages:
Intermediate and Advanced

Subjects:
Creative Writing, Drawing, Drama, and Science

During the 1930s, Sinclair Oil "adopted" a dinosaur as their trademark. The ancient beast, they felt, was a great way to symbolize their claim that "the oldest crudes make the finest lubes." Other companies—from tool manufacturers to moving companies—have also used dinosaurs in advertising.

Here's an activity that will give your group a chance to create their own dinosaur ads. Divide your group into smaller groups of three or four and tell them to pretend they are advertisers who have been hired to promote a product. Dinosaurs, or some aspect of the dinosaurs' lives, must be the focal point of the ad the kids come up with.

Either you can assign each group a product and a dinosaur-related concept or you can let the kids come up with their own. To present their ads, the groups can create posters, complete with slogans and artwork. Or they can make up television commercials and perform them in front of the other kids.

Here are a few examples of the kinds of ad slogans dinosaurs could stimulate:
- Don't get stuck with a fossil—buy MBI Computer Products for the latest in home computer technology!
- Attention, all you heavy-duty meat eaters! Come to the grand opening of the Carnosaur Cafe! Our menu has 47 all-meat dishes.

Dinovision

The great rock and roll channel—1001

What If . . . ?

Write a story about a dinosaur "what if?" situation.

Objective:
Write a creative dinosaur story.

Ages:
Intermediate and Advanced

Materials:
* *copies of page 49 (optional)*

Subjects:
Science and Creative Writing

hat would happen if the dinosaurs had never died out? Or if they suddenly made a comeback? What would you do if you found a baby hadrosaur on your doorstep one morning?

Children like to think about "what if" situations like these—it gives them a chance to really use their imaginations. In this creative writing activity they can put their imaginings down on paper. Assign the kids (or have them make up) a "what if" topic to write a story about. Here are some suggestions:

What if . . .
* you were shipwrecked on an island of dinosaurs
* you made the first dinosaur discovery
* the dinosaurs hadn't become extinct
* you were accidentally locked in a dinosaur museum overnight
* you built a time machine and went back to the Cretaceous Period
* you drank a potion that turned you into a dinosaur
* the dinosaurs reappeared
* you found a baby dinosaur
* the dinosaurs had never existed (How would life be different today?)
* you found a big egg, kept it warm, and a dinosaur hatched from it.

Use copies of page 49 as another creative writing activity. Have the kids cut out the pictures and rearrange them in any order to make up a story or comic strip. Then have each person share his or her story with the rest of the group.

COPYCAT PAGE

Turn this jumble of pictures into a story! You can write about the pictures in any order you like—just make sure your story includes what's happening in each one.

Rocky cliff

Thunderstorm

Pteranodon

Tyrannosaurus

Herd of hadrosaurs

Waterhole

Volcanic eruption

Triceratops

Triceratops eggs hatching

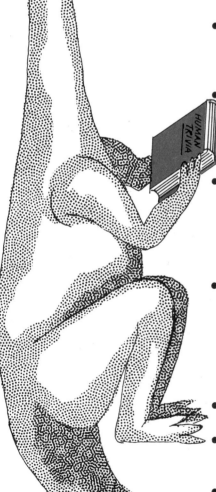

- Dinosaurs were the rulers of the earth for over 100 million years—about 20 times as long as people have been around.
- *Compsognathus* was one of the very smallest dinosaurs. It was only about as big as a chicken.
- The huge flying reptile known as *Quetzacoatlus* had a wingspan of over 40 feet (12 m)—four times as large as the largest wingspan among modern birds.
- One of the largest fossil bones ever found is a nine-foot (2.7-m) shoulder bone belonging to *Ultrasaurus*. The complete dinosaur may have been 45 feet (14 m) tall and 85 feet (26 m) long. And it weighed 80 tons (72 t)—as much as 15 African elephants!
- The brain of *Apatosaurus* made up only 1/100,000 of its body weight.
- How would you like to live in a town called Dinosaur? Dinosaur, Colorado, even has streets named Allosaurus Alley, Trachodon Terrace, and Stegosaurus Street.
- After spending three years digging up dinosaur remains in Africa, members of a German expedition shipped home 250 tons (225 t) of fossils!
- To successfully attack *Ankylosaurus*, a hungry carnosaur had to flip the heavily armored dinosaur on its back. That's not easy when your victim weighs five tons (4.5 t)!
- One of the strangest fossil discoveries was unearthed in 1971. It was the remains of a *Protoceratops* and a *Velociraptor* in mortal combat, with the carnivorous *Velociraptor* still gripping the *Protoceratops's* frill with its claws.
- The "sail" on the back of *Spinosaurus* probably helped this dinosaur regulate its body temperature. When it was too hot, *Spinosaurus* turned its sail away from the sun to lose heat. To warm up after a cold night, the dinosaur turned its sail toward the sun.
- Some scientists believe that certain dinosaurs bellowed like crocodiles.
- The daily diet of an *Apatosaurus* may have consisted of as much as 1¾ tons (1.5 t) of plants.
- The oldest known fossil, one of blue-green algae, was found in rocks some 3400 million years old.
- The largest dinosaur eggs were found in southern France. They are the size of basketballs and were probably laid by a large sauropod called *Hypselosaurus.*
- *Iguanodon* used the spikes on its thumbs to drive away predators—but early paleontologists thought the animal's spikes belonged on its nose.
- There were so many dinosaur bones lying on the ground near Medicine Bow, Wyoming, that a shepherd made a cabin out of them!
- The dinosaur known as *Ouranosaurus* lived in what is now the Sahara Desert. Sand can blow so fiercely there that it wears away the rock where fossilized *Ouranosaurus* skeletons are embedded. Scientists can sometimes find these skeletons lying on the dunes—as if the dinosaurs had died recently!
- *Tyrannosaurus's* front arms were so short that they couldn't reach its mouth.
- Paleontologists have found that some dinosaurs suffered from arthritis, bone cancer, tumors, and other diseases.
- *Tanystropheus* was a huge fish-eating reptile with a superlong neck. Its body was only 3½ feet (1 m) long, but its neck stretched over 10 feet (3 m).
- *Pachycephalosaurus*, the "thick-headed lizard," looked like a creature from another planet. It had a nine-inch (22.5 cm) thick skull and its head was covered with wartlike bumps.
- One of the smallest dinosaur skeletons ever found was the size of a robin. It was the skeleton of a baby *Mussaurus*, or "mouse lizard."
- Twenty-one of Great Britain's leading scientists ate dinner inside an *Iguanodon* model during the building of the dinosaur exhibit at the Crystal Palace, New Year's Eve, 1853.
- Dinosaur fossils have been found on every continent.

```
        J E S      O
   U E W  M L O  S T S
   L L A M E (T E E T H) H T A     L
   I H I L L A M S U M N E B E A N
   H E N S E K I P S E A I M T C
   J E H K R L Q U E C S D U E W   O T
   M O N R C A I P O U K A G S O O E B H
   L N V S D R N S R C I X A E L F L E O
    I O T V S O N A D E S P U E T O A T
   W O S M I O M G R G I H T Y M D A N S T N
   P O N E D L R T O B N A N C L A S G N S A N
    A O S F F L Z H E O L A T I N F E I T I B A
   K W O L O D L M I A S K N L O O S H R C O T L E P
    I T N P L A T E S   M I   O P N   T S A F E U M S O
   E C R O T A T R     O W   T Y E   E J A E B A T R P
   R A T T I M        R A   A O S   G K F P
 P S G G E            T L   E L T   Q S
 G V                  S C   M K S T  Q U A
                                     E S I
```

Directions:
Use the clues below to find the dinosaur words hidden in the *Stegosaurus*. The words may read frontward, backward, up, down, and diagonally.

1. *Tyrannosaurus,* a fierce meat eater, had many sharp T E E T H.
2. Dinosaur young hatched from _ _ _ _.
3. Scientists dig up _ _ _ _ _ _ _ to see what dinosaurs looked like.
4. *Apatosaurus* used its long _ _ _ _ to reach the tops of trees.
5. The three long _ _ _ _ _ on *Triceratops's* face kept away unfriendly dinosaurs.
6. When dinosaurs walked in mud some of them left _ _ _ _ _ _ that we can find today.
7. Dinosaurs with small teeth that looked like pegs ate _ _ _ _ _ _ _ .
8. *Apatosaurus* was 70 _ _ _ _ (21 m) long—that's the length of two school buses parked one in front of the other!
9. *Ankylosaurus's* bony _ _ _ _ _ _ protected it from other dinosaurs.
10. Some dinosaurs laid their eggs in large _ _ _ _ _ .
11. Many meat-eating dinosaurs had very sharp _ _ _ _ _ _ on their hands and feet for ripping their prey.
12. Many dinosaurs lived in _ _ _ _ _ as protection from enemies.
13. *Stegosaurus* used the _ _ _ _ _ _ on its tail to keep away hungry predators like *Allosaurus.*
14. Some scientists think many dinosaurs lived much _ _ _ _ _ _ than people do.
15. Many dinosaur names are made up of Greek and _ _ _ _ _ words.
16. The last dinosaurs all died out 65 _ _ _ _ _ _ _ years ago.
17. If you want to see dinosaurs today, you can go to a _ _ _ _ _ _ _.
18. Not all dinosaurs were slow—some could run very _ _ _ _.
19. Dinosaurs with teeth as sharp as knives ate _ _ _ _.

51

CRAFTY CORNER

Here are some dinosaur art and craft ideas you can use to complement many of the activities in the first five sections.

Build a Box-O-Saurus

Build a collection of dinosaurs using different-sized boxes.

Ages:
Primary and Intermediate

Materials:
- *small empty boxes (from toothpaste, film, cereal, gelatin, aspirin, and other household products)*
- *glue*
- *paper egg cartons (optional)*
- *tempera paint*
- *white paper*
- *liquid detergent (optional)*

Subject:
Crafts

Have your group bring in small empty boxes to build their own boxy beasts. Here's how to make a *Tyrannosaurus*:

Cut a toothpaste box off at an angle and glue it to a larger box to form the *Tyrannosaurus*'s neck and body (see diagram). For the head, use a smaller box such as an empty film box or cut off part of another toothpaste box. Cut the box at an angle as before and glue the box to the end of the neck.

For the legs, use sections of a paper egg carton or just cut legs from the side of another box. Then cover the entire dinosaur with paper and paint it. (You can paint the dinosaur without covering it with paper, but add a few drops of liquid detergent to the tempera so that it will stick.)

With a little imagination you can make other boxy dinosaurs too. Why not create a whole Mesozoic scene with them? You can even make a tree fern out of egg cartons: Just cut the pillars from the middle of a carton, stack them, and glue them together to form a trunk (see diagram). Then cut the leaves from the top of the carton and paint the tree fern different shades of green and brown.

Dinosaur Stick-Ups

Make colorful paper dinosaur stickers.

Ages:
Primary and Intermediate

(continued next page)

Dinosaur stick-ups are easy to make and fun to decorate with. Here's how to make these colorful stickers:
1) Run off copies of page 43 and give each person his or her own page of dinosaurs.
2) Have the children cut the dinosaurs from the page. (They can try to cut along the lines or just cut the approximate shapes, leaving a small border around each one.)
4) To make the sticky stuff, heat one envelope of unflavored gelatin with one cup of water over medium heat. Heat until all the gelatin dissolves. (For larger groups

use two envelopes and two cups of water.)

5) Pour the liquid into several containers placed around the room. Tell the kids to use their paintbrushes to lightly cover the backs of their stickers with the liquid. Remind them to use only a thin layer of gelatin. (As they "paint," also remind them to be careful of the gelatin mixture because it stays hot for a long time.)

Explain that they should try not to get any of the gelatin on the "face down" side of the stickers because the gelatin keeps the paper from coloring well later.

Let the stickers dry completely for one to two hours.

6) When the stickers are dry, get out the markers, colored pencils, or crayons. Since no one really knows for sure what color the dinosaurs were, tell the kids to use all the colors of the rainbow to make bright, colorful stickers.

When the stickers are all set to stick, tell the group to give the backs a lick and then press them to a surface. These dinosaurs stick to paper best but will also stick to metal and other smooth surfaces. (To store the "unlicked" stickers, keep them between two pieces of wax paper until ready to use.)

Boning Up on Dinosaurs

Build a life-sized dinosaur bone using paper-mache and chicken wire.

When you're talking about *Apatosaurus* bones, you're talking big! For example, an individual vertebra can measure three feet (90 cm) from tip to tip. And the femur could get to be over six feet (1.8 m) long.

In this activity, your group can build an *Apatosaurus* femur out of paper-mache to get a feeling for the size of these giant sauropods. Before starting, show your group a picture of *Apatosaurus*. (Since it's one of the best-known dinosaurs, most dinosaur books have a picture of it. But while you're checking for pictures, keep in mind that *Apatosaurus* was once known as *Brontosaurus*.) Make sure your children

Bruce Norfleet

know which bone you're talking about when you say "femur." Have them point to their own femurs. (It's the bone between the hip and the knee.) Explain that an *Apatosaurus* femur is about five times the size of a human femur.

Here's how to build the bone:

1) First find a large working area. Outside is best. But you can also build this monstrous bone in a corner of the cafeteria, in a basement work area, or at the back of a classroom. If you work inside, cover the work area with plastic to protect the floor. NOTE: On the days before you work on the bone, make sure you tell your group to wear old clothes or to bring in painting aprons. Paper-mache paste can get all over everything (but easily washes out of most fabrics).

2) Form the length of the bone with chicken wire. To do this have the children roll the wire into a long cylinder with an 8-inch (20-cm) diameter. Then clip off the excess exposed wire at the end openings.

3) Stuff the cylinder with balls of tightly wadded newspaper. (This will give it support when the paper-mache is applied.) Be sure to caution the children to be very careful of sharp ends when handling the wire. You might suggest that they wear garden gloves when rolling it into a cylinder.

4) When the bone is stuffed, twist the ends of the wire together in a dozen or so places

(continued next page)

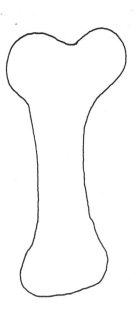

with twist ties or pipe cleaner halves. Then use wire cutters to clip off exposed wire ends.

5) To make the ends of the bone look like a real bone (see diagram), tape two large pieces of balled-up newspaper to one end and one even larger ball to the other.

6) Now you're ready to make the paste and cut up the newspaper. Have one group mix the flour and water in a large washtub or bucket. To do one whole side, you will need to combine 5 pounds (2.3 kg) of flour with 10 cups (2.4 l) of warm water. Mix the flour and water until a smooth paste forms, and then pour the concoction into smaller buckets. Have the other group cut the newspaper into strips 6-8 inches (15-20 cm) long and 3-4 inches (8-10 cm) wide.

7) Lay the bone on two chairs (one supporting each end). Then have the children work in shifts to cover the top half of the wire cylinder with paper-mache.

8) Let the first layer dry for a few days, and then turn it over and work on the other side.

9) For a final layer, apply strips of paper towels (the institutional kind) to give the bone a smooth look and a boney color. (You can also paint the bone when it dries.)

Once the bone is dry, have all the "bonemakers" sign their creation with markers. Then put the bone on display for others to see. You can also display a chicken femur (thighbone) next to the dinosaur femur for comparison. It's a mighty big difference!

Prehistoric Pop-Up Cards

Cut, paste, and color dinosaur pop-up cards.

Ages:
Intermediate and Advanced

Materials:
- *copies of page 55*
- *crayons*
- *lightweight cardboard*
- *rulers*
- *scissors*

Subject:
Arts and Crafts

Your group can make a scene from the Mesozoic spring into life when they put together Prehistoric Pop-up Cards. First pass out pieces of lightweight cardboard and copies of page 55. Have the kids color the background and the *Triceratops,* then cut both pictures out along the dark solid lines. Tell them to fold on all the dotted lines.

Next have the kids cut their cardboard into 6½ x 9-inch (16.5 x 23-cm) cards. On each of the 9-inch (23-cm) sides, they should mark a point 4½ inches (11.5 cm) from the ends. Then have them draw a line between the two points, marking the center

of the card. Have them fold the card along the line. (To make the cardboard easier to fold, just hold a ruler to one side of the line. Then pull the pointed end of a pair of scissors along the ruler, making a crease in the center of the card.)

Now tell the kids to mark points 2¾ inches (7 cm) and 4 inches (10 cm) from the top edge of their cards, on the middle line. Have them glue or tape the bottom flaps of the background to the card, making sure the center of the background is at the 2¾-inch (7-cm) mark. Each end of the background should be about ¾ inch (2 cm) from the top edge of the card. (The end will be at an angle to the top of the card. See diagram.) Now they can glue or tape the *Triceratops* to the card at the 4-inch (10-cm) mark. They should arrange it at an angle similar to that of the background.

Your group may want to decorate the flat area around their pop-up dinosaur scenes by coloring in ferns, rocks, or whatever comes to mind. Or they could write a verse about their creations in the blank space. Some may even decide to jot a note inside their cards and send them to someone special.

Idea for pop-up cards reprinted with permission from *Never a Dull Moment* by Sue Tarsky, Schocken Books, published by Pantheon Books, a division of Random House, Inc.

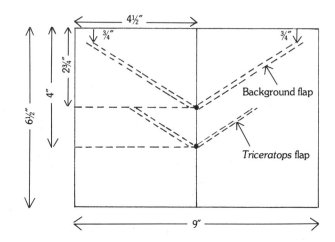

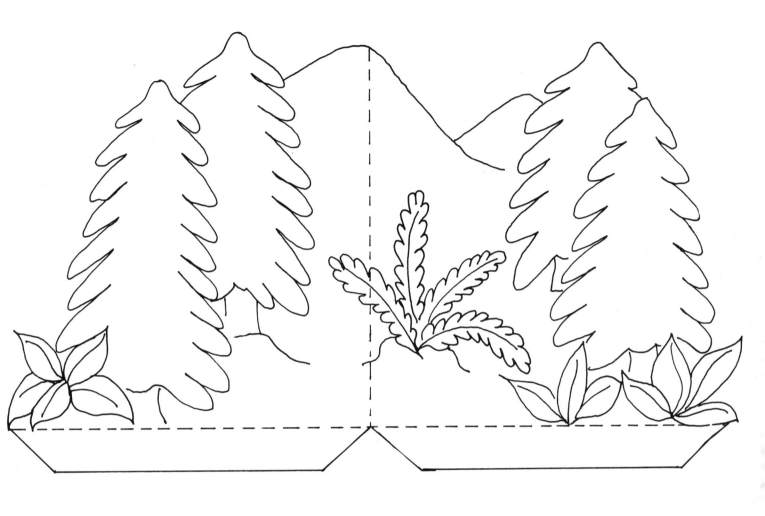

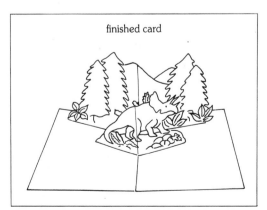

finished card

APPENDIX

WHERE TO SEE DINOSAURS

Note: Arrange tours at least four to six weeks in advance. The museums are busiest in the spring—if that's when you want to go, make your reservations as early as possible.

UNITED STATES

American Museum of Natural History, New York, New York. If notified two weeks in advance, an educator from the education department will lead your tour (for New York residents only). Telephone (212) 769-5304.

Carnegie Museum of Natural History, Pittsburgh, Pennsylvania. Special dinosaur tours are available throughout the year. Telephone (412) 622-3289.

Cleveland Museum of Natural History, Cleveland, Ohio. Offers programs on dinosaurs during the school year. Telephone (216) 231-8002.

Dinosaur National Monument, near Jensen, Utah. Offers a variety of scheduled programs. Write to Dinosaur National Monument, Box 128, Jensen, UT 84035.

Dinosaur State Park, Rocky Hill, Connecticut. Features dinosaur models and fossilized tracks. If you bring your own materials you can make casts from the tracks. Telephone (203) 529-8423.

Field House of Natural History State Park, Vernal, Utah. Offers self-guided tours and features a dinosaur garden with more than a dozen life-sized replicas. Telephone (801) 789-4002.

Field Museum of Natural History, Chicago, Illinois. Programs on dinosaurs and other prehistoric life are available for grades 4-12. Telephone (312) 922-9410 ext. 353 for tour request form.

George C. Page Museum of La Brea Discoveries, Los Angeles, California. Although no dinosaurs are shown in this tour, you can see the remains of saber-toothed cats, mammoths, and giant sloths taken from the La Brea Tar Pits. Telephone (213) 857-6306; call Wednesday through Friday, 1-4 pm.

Las Vegas Natural History Museum, Las Vegas, Nevada. Offers tours on dinosaurs and other prehistoric life. Telephone (702) 798-7757.

National Museum of Natural History, Washington, D.C. Tours are offered on prehistoric life (with an emphasis on dinosaurs if the teacher requests) for all grade levels. Teacher workshops on dinosaurs are also available. Telephone (202) 357-2747.

Natural History Museum of Los Angeles County, California. Features a dinosaur exhibit. Tours are offered during the school year. Telephone (213) 744-3333.

Pratt Museum of Natural History, Amherst College, Amherst, Massachusetts. Has a special dinosaur track exhibit for tour groups. Tours are geared to the ages of the people in your group. Closed during summer months. Telephone (413) 542-2165.

Utah Museum of Natural History, University of Utah, Salt Lake City, Utah. General or specialized tours are available. Telephone (801) 581-4887.

CANADA

Dinosaur Provincial Park, Brooks, Alberta. A U.N.E.S.C.O. World Heritage Site. Several dinosaurs on display. Guided tours to excavation sites during the summer. Telephone (403) 378-4587.

Museum of Natural Science, Ottawa, Ontario. Offers guided tours October through April. Telephone (613) 992-4260.

Royal Ontario Museum, Toronto, Ontario. Tours are available for grades 4 and up. Telephone (416) 586-5801.

Tyrrell Museum of Palaeontology, Drumheller, Alberta. General and student tours are offered. Telephone (403) 823-7707.

This is only a partial list. If you live near a natural history museum we haven't listed, check to see whether dinosaur tours are available. There may also be a dinosaur park in your area with life-sized models for the children to see.

DID SOME DINOSAURS HAVE FEATHERS?

More than a hundred years ago a "new" fossil creature was discovered that looked partly like a bird and partly like a dinosaur. It was about the size of a crow and had wings and feathers like a bird's. But it also had a long, dinosaurlike tail and many sharp teeth in its beak. (Unlike a dinosaur's tail, which is made up of vertebrae, a bird's tail is mostly feathers. Also, modern birds don't have true teeth.) Scientists called this strange feathered creature *Archaeopteryx*, which means "ancient wing."

Was *Archaeopteryx* one of the first birds? Most scientists think so. But others think it was a tiny, fast-moving dinosaur with feathers and wings. They think it ran along the ground catching insects and taking short flying spurts off the ground.

Whether it was a bird or a dinosaur, *Archaeopteryx* does show us that birds and dinosaurs are very closely related. In fact, many scientists are confident that the birds we see today are feathered descendents of the dinosaurs.

WERE THE DINOSAURS WARM-BLOODED OR COLD-BLOODED?

For more than a hundred years, scientists thought all of the dinosaurs were cold-blooded animals. But today some scientists think that at least some of the dinosaurs may have been warm-blooded. Here are a few facts that seem to support the possibility that dinosaurs were warm-blooded:

- *Speed:* Many of the dinosaurs were built for speed. Some might have run faster than a horse. Many scientists think that only warm-blooded animals have enough energy to run fast.
- *Big Brains:* Many dinosaurs had large brains in relation to their body sizes. This is a characteristic of warm-blooded, not cold-blooded, animals.
- *Predators and Prey:* Warm-blooded predators, such as tigers, need a lot of food to keep them alive. But cold-blooded predators don't. (For example, a crocodile needs only one-eighth as much food as a tiger needs per pound of body weight.) Scientists have found many more fossils of dinosaur prey than of dinosaur predators. This ratio of predators to prey is similar to predator/prey ratios of warm-blooded animals.

Another suggestion is that some of the largest dinosaurs were *passively* warm-blooded. That means they couldn't control their body temperatures as true warm-blooded animals can. But they did manage to keep a constant body temperature most of the time because their bodies were so big. Scientists say it took them so long to heat up and cool down that they usually just stayed about the same temperature.

Many paleontologists disagree with these ideas, claiming there isn't enough evidence yet to support them. Others think that only some of the smaller, more agile dinosaurs were warm-blooded and the rest were cold-blooded.

WHAT HAPPENED TO THE DINOSAURS?

It's a sure bet that this question will come up in any conversation about dinosaurs. A lot of speculations about the extinction of the dinosaurs have been made based on the few clues unearthed by paleontologists. Here are a few ideas:

- Since they had such small brains, dinosaurs were too stupid to adapt to a changing world.
- Plants that the dinosaurs ate died out and, unable to adapt to another food source, the plant eaters starved. With no prey, the predatory dinosaurs soon did the same.
- A surge of volcanic activity destroyed the earth's ozone layer and allowed too much deadly ultraviolet radiation from the sun to reach the earth's surface.
- A severe drop in temperature killed the dinosaurs because they weren't insulated from the cold.
- The seas receded and reduced the amount of marine algae that absorbed carbon dioxide. This caused a buildup of CO_2 in the atmosphere and made the overall temperature of the earth rise. Dinosaurs couldn't adapt to the heat.
- A star exploded and sent out huge amounts of radiation. This caused the death of marine life, the thinning of dinosaur eggshells, and other changes.
- A huge asteroid collided with the earth, covering it with a dust cloud that blocked the sun for years. It destroyed most of the plant life, and the dinosaurs starved. Only small animals survived until the cloud dispersed.
- A shower of comets pelted the earth, having the same effect as an asteroid would have had, stirring up dust and blocking out the sun.

Glossary

amphibian—an animal that usually spends its immature life in the water but lives on land as an adult.

bird-hipped dinosaurs—one of the two orders of dinosaurs, named because the pelvis (hipbone) resembles that of birds. Most were plant eaters with beaklike jaws. (The scientific name for the order is *Ornithischia*.

carnivorous—eating meat exclusively.

carnosaurs—a group of lizard-hipped, meat-eating dinosaurs. They were powerful predators with massive heads and daggerlike teeth. A good example of a carnosaur is *Tyrannosaurus*.

Cenozoic Era—a major geologic time division that started 65 million years B.P. and continues today. Also called the Age of Mammals.

cold-blooded—a cold-blooded animal cannot internally control its body temperature. Its temperature changes as the surrounding temperature goes up and down. Insects, fish, amphibians, and reptiles are cold-blooded.

continental drift—term used to describe the slow movements of the earth's continents.

Cretaceous Period—the last period of the Mesozoic Era. During this period the dinosaurs reached their peak, then became extinct. Birds and small mammals were common.

fossils—the remains or evidence of ancient organisms preserved in rock or some other material.

hadrosaurs—a group of bird-hipped, plant-eating dinosaurs. Also known as duck-billed dinosaurs because of their wide beaks. Many had strange crests on their heads. A good example of a hadrosaur is *Edmontosaurus* (*Anatosaurus*).

herbivorous—eating plants exclusively.

invertebrate—an animal without a backbone.

Jurassic Period—the second period of the Mesozoic Era. During this period the first birds appeared. Dinosaurs were abundant.

lizard-hipped dinosaurs—one of the two orders of dinosaurs, named because the pelvis (hipbone) resembles that of lizards. This order contains both plant-eating and meat-eating dinosaurs. (The scientific name for the order is *Saurischia*.)

Mesozoic Era—a major geologic time division that lasted from 245 million to 65 million years B.P. Also called the Age of Dinosaurs. It is made up of the Triassic, Jurassic, and Cretaceous Periods.

mammals—a class of vertebrates that feed their young milk secreted from mammary glands and have skin that is usually covered with hair.

omnivorous—eating both plants and meat.

paleontology—the study of ancient life. A *paleontologist* is a scientist who is trained in both geology and biology and who studies fossil records to learn about life of the past.

Paleozoic Era—a major geological time divison that lasted from 600 million to 245 million B.P. Also called the Age of Ancient Life. In this era, reptiles, fish, land and sea plants, and amphibians evolved.

Pangaea—super-continent that formed in the Permian Period of the Paleozoic Era. All the land masses were part of this super-continent. Pangaea stayed together until the Triassic Period in the Mesozoic Era, when it began to split up into the continents we know today.

reptiles—a class of vertebrates that usually lays eggs on land and have lungs when they are born. Includes present-day turtles, snakes, lizards, and crocodiles.

sauropods—a group of lizard-hipped, plant-eating dinosaurs. They had long necks for browsing on the highest leaves. The massive sauropods were among the largest animals ever to have lived. A good example of a sauropod is *Apatosaurus* (also known as *Brontosaurus*.)

Triassic Period—the first period of the Mesozoic Era. During this period the dinosaurs and mammals first evolved.

vertebrate—an animal with a backbone.

warm-blooded—a warm-blooded animal can maintain a constant body temperature, using energy from the food it eats. Birds and mammals are warm-blooded.

Questions, Questions, and More Questions

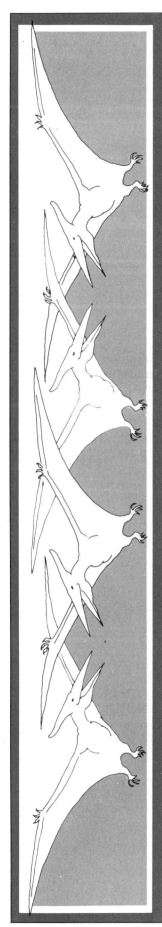

1. Name the three most recent geologic eras. (Paleozoic, Mesozoic, and Cenozoic)
2. True or false: Scientists estimate that dinosaurs were around for about 500 to 1000 years. (False. Dinosaurs were around for nearly 160 million years.)
3. Which era do we live in? (the Cenozoic)
4. True or false: Dinosaur fossils have been found in North America and Africa only. (False. Dinosaur fossils have been found on every continent.)
5. Did the last Ice Age occur before or after the Age of Dinosaurs? (after)
6. True or false: Some dinosaurs probably lived in herds as deer do. (True)
7. What does the word "dinosaur" mean? (terrible lizard)
8. True or false: Early humans hunted certain dinosaurs for food. (False. Dinosaurs had been extinct for about 60 million years before people evolved.)
9. In which era did the dinosaurs live? (the Mesozoic)
10. True or false: Some dinosaurs walked on all four feet and others walked on two feet. (True)
11. Name one theory that explains why the dinosaurs became extinct. (See page 57 for a list.)
12. True or false: Some dinosaurs had fur. (False. Skin impressions for each of the major groups of dinosaurs show a pebbly texture, but no evidence of fur.)
13. What is a fossil? (the remains or evidence of ancient organisms preserved in rock or some other material)
14. True or false: At the time of the dinosaurs, the continents were in pretty much the same positions as they are today. (False. At the beginning of the Age of Dinosaurs, the continents were together in one big landmass and were just starting to break up.)
15. Name two plant-eating dinosaurs. (*Apatosaurus, Stegosaurus, Diplodocus, Ankylosaurus, Hadrosaurus,* and others)
16. True or false: Dinosaurs were reptiles. (True)
17. Name two meat-eating dinosaurs. (*Tyrannosaurus, Allosaurus, Acrocanthosaurus, Compsognathus, Megalosaurus, Ornitholestes,* and others)
18. True or false: The huge flying reptiles called pterosaurs were *not* dinosaurs. (True)
19. According to scientists, how might some of the dinosaurs have attracted mates? (by calling and/or showing brightly colored crests or throat patches)
20. True or false: Elephants are descended from some of the largest dinosaurs. (False. Elephants are mammals. Dinosaurs were reptiles.)
21. Give an example of a dinosaur name and what it means. (See chart on pages 60-61.)
22. True or false: Some dinosaurs probably hunted in packs as wolves do. (True)
23. Name two kinds of animals that lived during the Age of Dinosaurs that were *not* dinosaurs. (pterosaurs, plesiosaurs, cockroaches, shrewlike mammals, birds, and others)
24. Dinosaur names are made up of words that come from which two languages? (Greek and Latin)
25. True or false: Some dinosaurs were meat eaters, some were plant eaters, and some ate both meat and plants. (True)
26. Which of these groups of animals—amphibians, birds, or reptiles—are thought to be descended from dinosaurs? (birds)
27. True or false: All dinosaurs were bigger than a full-grown moose. (False. Some, like the chicken-sized *Compsognathus,* were very small.)
28. What is a scientist who studies fossils called? (a paleontologist)
29. True or false: Some dinosaurs may have been warm-blooded. (True)
30. What do scientists call the giant landmass that all of the continents were part of at the beginning of the Age of Dinosaurs? (Pangaea)
31. True or false: Some dinosaurs probably lived their whole lives in the sea. (False. So far no fossils of water-dwelling dinosaurs have been found.)
32. True or false: Some dinosaurs were amphibians, some were reptiles, and a few were mammals. (False. All dinosaurs were reptiles.)
33. True or false: Trilobites were some of the earliest dinosaurs. (False. Trilobites were a type of marine invertebrate that lived in the Paleozoic Era.)
34. True or false: All dinosaurs were vertebrates. (True)
35. True or false: Most dinosaurs ate both plants and meat. (False. Most dinosaurs were either meat eaters or plant eaters. A few dinosaurs ate both types of food.)

THE DINOSAUR CHART

Dinosaur Name and Pronunciation	Meaning	Where Fossils Have Been Found	Food	Length	Weight	Fascinating Facts
Acrocanthosaurus (AK-ro-KANTH-uh-SAWR-us)	"very spiny lizard"	United States (OK)	meat	40 ft. (12 m)	4-5 tons (3.7-4.5 t)	A long row of spines ran down Acrocanthosaurus's back. Some of these spines were 12 inches (30 cm) long!
Allosaurus (AL-uh-SAWR-us)	"other lizard"	United States (CO, WY, UT)	meat	36 ft. (11 m)	2-3 tons (1.8-2.7 t)	The remains of more than 40 allosaurs have been collected from a single area in Utah.
Ammosaurus (AM-uh-SAWR-us)	"sand lizard"	Canada (Nova Scotia) and United States (AZ, MA)	plants	8 ft. (2.4 m)	85 lb. (38 kg)	Ammosaurus may sometimes have walked on its hind legs and sometimes on all four feet.
Ankylosaurus (ang-kile-uh-SAWR-us)	"curved lizard"	Canada (Alberta) and United States (MT)	plants	17 ft. (5 m)	5 tons (4.5 t)	A blow from Ankylosaurus's club-like tail may have been powerful enough to break a predator's leg.
Apatosaurus (ah-PAT-uh-SAWR-us)	"deceptive lizard"	United States (CO, OK, UT, WY)	plants	70 ft. (21 m)	25-33 tons (23-30 t)	Apatosaurus weighed as much as five African elephants!
Brachiosaurus (BRAK-ee-uh-SAWR-us)	"arm lizard"	Africa (Tanzania) and United States (CO)	plants	75 ft. (22 m)	75 tons (68 t)	Brachiosaurus is one of the largest known land animals.
Coelophysis (see-lo-FISE-iss)	"hollow form"	United States (AZ, NM, TX)	meat	10 ft. (3 m)	65 lb. (29 kg)	Coelophysis had hollow bones as birds do today.
Compsognathus (komp-sug-NAY-thus)	"pretty jaws"	Europe (France and West Germany)	meat	2 ft. (60 cm)	6 lbs. (2.7 kg)	Compsognathus was about the size of a chicken.
Corythosaurus (ko-RITH-uh-SAWR-us)	"helmet lizard"	Canada (Alberta)	meat	23 ft. (7 m)	3-4 tons (2.7-3.6 t)	Corythosaurus was one of the duck-billed dinosaurs with an unusual crest on its head.
Daspletosaurus (dass-PLEE-tuh-SAWR-us)	"frightful lizard"	Canada (Alberta)	meat	28 ft. (8.4 m)	3.5 tons (3.2 t)	Daspletosaurus was a cousin of Tyrannosaurus.
Deinonychus (dine-ON-ik-us)	"terrible claw"	United States (MT, UT)	meat	9 ft. (2.7 m)	175 lb. (79 kg)	Deinonychus had a big, sickle-shaped claw for attacking prey.
Diplodocus (dih-PLOD-uh-kus)	"double beam"	United States (CO, MT, UT, WY)	plants	88 ft. (26 m)	11.7 tons (10.5 t)	Diplodocus had a hole near the top of its skull which may have helped it breathe while feeding.
Edmontosaurus (ed-MONT-uh-SAWR-us)	"Edmonton lizard"	Canada (Alberta) and United States (MT, NJ, WY)	plants	43 ft. (13 m)	3.4 tons (3.1 t)	Mummified specimens of Edmontosaurus show that it had a fleshy crest along its back and tail.
Hadrosaurus (HAD-ro-SAWR-us)	"big lizard"	United States (NJ)	plants	30 ft. (9 m)	3 tons (2.7 t)	Hadrosaurus was the first dinosaur to be discovered and recorded in North America.
Megalosaurus (MEG-ah-lo-SAWR-us)	"great lizard"	Europe (France and Great Britain)	meat	30 ft. (9 m)	3 tons (2.7 t)	Megalosaurus was the first dinosaur to be described.

Name (pronunciation)	Meaning	Location	Diet	Length	Weight	Description
(no-doe-SAWR-us)		(WY)		(5.4 m)	(1.8 t)	as did its relative, *Ankylosaurus*.
Ornitholestes (or-nith-o-LES-tees)	"bird robber"	United States (WY)	meat	6 ft. (1.8 m)	35 lb. (16 kg)	*Ornitholestes* was an agile, quick-moving dinosaur.
Ornithomimus (or-nith-o-MY-mus)	"bird mimic"	Canada (Alberta) and United States (MT, WY)	both	11½ ft. (3.5 m)	300 lb. (135 kg)	*Ornithomimus* looked a lot like an ostrich.
Pachycephalosaurus (pak-ee-SEF-uh-lo-SAWR-us)	"thick-headed lizard"	Canada (Alberta, Saskatchewan) and United States (MT, WY)	plants	15 ft. (4.5 m)	500 lb. (225 kg)	*Pachycephalosaurus* was a bone-headed dinosaur. Rival males may have butted heads together as bighorn sheep do today.
Protoceratops (pro-toe-SAIR-uh-tops)	"first horned face"	Asia (Mongolia and China)	plants	6 ft. (1.8 m)	150 lb. (68 kg)	*Protoceratops* was the first dinosaur for which eggs were found.
Psittacosaurus (SIT-uh-ko-SAWR-us)	"parrot lizard"	Asia (China and Mongolia)	plants	2-5 ft. (60 cm-1.5 m)	50 lb. (22.5 kg)	A *Psittacosaurus* mother probably guarded her young.
Spinosaurus (SPY-no-SAWR-us)	"thorn lizard"	Africa (Egypt and Niger)	meat	40 ft. (12 m)	6 tons (5.4 t)	*Spinosaurus* had a sail on its back that was supported by spines that were 6 feet (1.8 m) long.
Stegosaurus (STEG-uh-SAWR-us)	"roof lizard"	United States (CO, OK, SD, UT, WY)	plants	30 ft. (9 m)	2 tons (1.8 t)	*Stegosaurus*'s brain was very small.
Troodon (true-OH-don)	"wound tooth"	Canada (Alberta) and United States (MT, WY)	meat	6½ ft. (2 m)	60-100 lb. (27-45 kg)	*Troodon* may have been the smartest dinosaur.
Triceratops (try-SAIR-uh-tops)	"three-horned face"	Canada (Alberta, Saskatchewan) and United States (MT, ND, SD, WY)	plants	30 ft. (9 m)	8 tons (7.2 t)	The horns above *Triceratops*'s eyes were as long as 40 inches (100 cm).
Tyrannosaurus (tye-RAN-uh-SAWR-us)	"tyrant lizard"	Canada (Alberta and Saskatchewan) and United States (MT, SD, ND, WY)	meat	43 ft. (13 m)	7 tons (6.3 t)	Some of *Tyrannosaurus*'s teeth measured over 6 inches (15 cm) long.
Ultrasaurus (UL-truh-SAWR-us)	"ultra lizard"	United States (CO)	plants	85 ft. (26 m) or more	possibly 80 tons (72 t)	*Ultrasaurus* is the largest dinosaur that's been discovered so far.

1997 Update

Table of Contents

No Bones About It
THE OTHER EVIDENCE OF DINOSAURS

S earching for evidence of prehistoric animals, especially dinosaurs, does not always mean looking for bones. Keys to the past are also revealed in other types of clues. Looking for and discovering these other signs of prehistoric life can increase the fun and excitement of hunting for fossils.

As everyone knows, fossils are evidence of prehistoric life. But, frequently, people think of fossils only as ancient bones that have turned to rock. In reality, fossils can be a variety of things, from impressions found in prehistoric mud caused by the impact of raindrops from a storm that occurred millions of years ago, all the way to the tracks of lumbering dinosaurs who strolled at the edge of an ancient lake bed. Fossils may include the remains of plants, eggs, even scat (or dung) . . . as well as the actual fossilized bones of prehistoric animals. The important thing to remember is that all this evidence contributes to our understanding of the ancient world.

Often, each piece of evidence depends on other, sometimes nearby, pieces of the ancient world preserved for our discovery.

Once Upon A Time at Picketwire

Along a remote riverbed in southern Colorado, ancient footprints from over 150 million years ago walk into the world we inhabit today. Here, the curious explorer can find the longest documented dinosaur trackway in the world. For over 700 feet, tracks left by a family of Jurassic-age dinosaurs are laid bare in the hardened sands of an ancient lakeshore.

Picketwire Canyon in Colorado, part of the Comanche National Grassland, contains over 1,300 dinosaur footprints that record the passage of individuals and also provide evidence of herd behavior in prehistoric animals. Scientists have identified over 100 different trackways there that can be followed on four separate levels of a prehistoric mud flat.

There are at least two major types of tracks revealed in these sediments. The first set is from a group of dinosaurs called sauropods or "lizard feet" (see figure A). A group of five apatosaurs (known also by their earlier name of brontosaurs) were probably traveling together along the edge of a lake as they moved north, perhaps in search of food.

The second group of dinosaur tracks found at Picketwire were made by carnivores, or meat-eaters, and were made by the three-toed allosaurs, a theropod or "beast feet" whose distinct trails are found right beside the apatosaurus' tracks (see figure B). Were they following the gentle plant-eating giants looking for an easy meal? We may never know for certain. But the evidence suggests that the tracks were made at about the same time.

Figure A
The tracks of the sauropod are hard to see. One scientist said they looked as if a giant stuck a telephone in the mud.

Scientists have determined that for every six plant-eating sauropods, there are four theropod tracks, a ratio of plant-eating animals to meat-eaters that is close to that found in large animal populations today.

Figure B
The meat-eating theropods left very distinct tracks. Note the claws at the end of the toes.

How Did Dinosaur Tracks Survive?

There are two theories about the preservation of fossil tracks or other impressions. The oldest idea is called the "cover-up" theory. According to this theory, a plant leaf, seed, or animal makes an impression in a relatively soft and moist material like sand or mud. The track print then dries and hardens in the sun, reducing the possibility of destruction. Next, a gradual deposit of softer material fills in the depression. Once buried, it remains protected. After the overlying softer material erodes away, it leaves the harder, rock impression of the fossil plant or animal behind. Often trackways go on for considerable distances. Once in a while, scientists following ancient footprints see them disappear—only to discover that if they remove the thin layers of softer rock just where the tracks seemed to vanish, they can find that the tracks continue.

The second theory of track preservation is that the weight of a passing dinosaur creates an impression under the surface of the land. This is a hidden or "ghost" track. Since it is already covered up, the footprint is much more likely to survive. But if the footprint was left in an underlying layer of mud much older that the surface, it might lead scientists to mistakenly assign an older age to the time the dinosaur lived (see figure C). So scientists gather as much information as possible to make the best possible guess about ancient life.

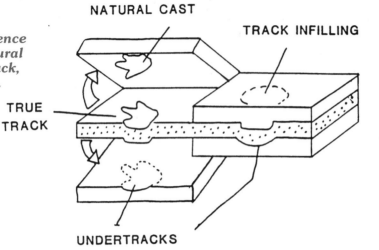

Figure C
This illustration shows the difference between the natural cast, the true track, and undertracks.

NATURAL CAST

TRACK INFILLING

TRUE TRACK

UNDERTRACKS

Footprints, the Footnotes to History

What can careful observation of dinosaur tracks tell us about the activity and prehistoric environment of the dinosaur? It can tell us if all animals passed at the same time, if there were more than two types of dinosaurs present, and how wet this landscape was in the prehistoric period.

It can suggest things about dinosaur sizes and habits, too. Are all the tracks about the same depth? Are they about the same size? Any consistency in the size and depth of tracks suggest that the animals who made them were about the same size.

If close observation tells you that the consistency and moisture content of the mud was about the same, all the animals probably made the tracks at the same time. Parallel tracks of different depths and size may suggest that they were made at different times, perhaps weeks or months apart.

Do Tracks "Talk"?

Trying to unravel the social behavior of prehistoric animals involves a great deal of speculation. But by studying tracks and comparing the animals we know today with the prehistoric ones, we may be able to reach a few conclusions.

A major question among scientists is whether early dinosaurs exhibited any herding instincts. Tracks that are evenly spaced suggest that animals were all moving together at the same time. The spacing of individual prehistoric animal tracks, when compared to the larger herding animals of today, like elephants or bison, reflect that some dinosaurs did travel in herds, or as a family unit. The tracks seem to maintain a constant distance between individuals walking together.

The relative size of tracks found together would reveal if they were all of the same age. If the tracks are of different sizes, perhaps they were a more mixed age group, such as a family of dinosaurs moving from one location to another, perhaps migrating to a better environment or looking for more abundant food.

Following dinosaur tracks for a distance may show evidence of all the animals turning at the same time to avoid soft mud or another obstacle such as a tree or rock. Tracks all moving in the same pattern is further evidence that all the dinosaurs may have passed a particular location at the same moment in time.

Occasionally, fossil records provide details that we might think are impossible to see after 150 million years. The trackway at Picketwire Canyon, for example, shows evidence of the trampling of freshwater clams by a passing herd of large sauropods. It pays to examine dinosaurs tracks closely because it may show details you never expected.

It may seem strange to you, but the discovery of dinosaur scat, called *coprolites*, has begun to provide scientists with additional information about dinosaurs, too. Several major problems exist in trying to interpret dinosaur scat because you can never be absolutely certain who left the evidence, unless, of course, other evidence like tracks or bones are found nearby.

Since the droppings are very soft, the environment may alter their size and shape. Also, once buried, the gradual transition from scat to rock takes a very long time. If the evidence contained in the scat is plant material (left by a plant-eater), or hair and bones (left by a meat-eater), it may decay before it can be preserved. Scientists thinly slice the fossil scat and examine it under a microscope. They have found small pieces of prehistoric pine trees and other plant remains, which tell us what the animals ate and also help us to understand what plants were around when dinosaurs roamed the earth.

Searching for Dinosaur Tracks and Other Evidence

While dinosaur tracks are not abundant, there are certain locations that are better than others for finding fossil evidence of dinosaurs.

Flat areas in river valleys have good potential for dinosaur tracks. Look at exposed road cuts, where road construction has shaved rock walls. Natural cliff faces and slopes are good places, too, to discover tracks as well as other fossil evidence. Because of the possible importance of the discoveries, you should report any new locations to a local paleontologist at a university.

Some of the places to see dinosaur tracks include Dinosaur State Park, Connecticut; Dinosaur State Park, Texas; Picketwire Canyon, Colorado; and a variety of locations in and around Moab, Utah. Who knows? Your explorations might even discover a new dinosaur trackway for others to see and enjoy! Good hunting.

EXCAVATING THE EVIDENCE

Do you think it would have been fun to live when dinosaurs roamed the earth? Things would certainly have been a lot different with animals that were the size of tractor trailers, tall buildings, or 200-year-old oak trees. But that's how big some of the dinosaurs were.

If dinosaurs were still here today, you might look out a high window in a tall building and find yourself nose to nose with an *Apatosaurus* standing outside on the ground! *Apatosaurus*, which means "deceptive lizard," was so tall it could rise up on its hind legs and look through a ninth-story window!

Or, if you lived out West, you might see a large fellow called *Triceratops* munching grass in your backyard. Plant-eater *Triceratops*, whose name means "three-horned face," looked very much like today's rhinoceros. Only it was more than three times bigger and had horns that were longer and stouter than baseball bats.

If dinosaurs were still here, you'd definitely want to stay out of the way of *Tyrannosaurus rex*, the ferocious "tyrant lizard." He was about the size of a two-story house, and had powerful hind feet with claws as long and sharp as steak knives and teeth like fierce rows of daggers. Meat-eater *Tyrannosaurus rex* walked around on two legs, not four, and he stalked easy to catch prey—which probably would have included people!

In reality, we will probably never see a live dinosaur. But the movie "Jurassic Park" gave us a fairly accurate idea of what life with them might have been like. In the film, scientists have discovered a way to extract genetic material from blood still lodged in the stomachs of Jurassic-age insects trapped in *amber* (fossilized tree sap). The scientists believe that because the insects fed on dinosaurs, the genetic matter, or DNA, must be from dinosaurs.

Next, genetically recreated dinosaurs start hatching out in the island laboratory of a somewhat misguided scientist. He plans to build a Disneyland-like theme park on the island that will house the greatest attraction of all time—live dinosaurs. He calls it Jurassic Park.

Opening day nears and invited guests begin to arrive. But suddenly things start going haywire. The dinosaurs go berserk and threaten to kill everybody. Disaster follows, as you know if you saw the movie.

But that's all too incredible, right? Well, for now it probably is. But there are other projects involving fossilized genetic matter indicating that one day such things may be possible. For instance, some scientists are said to be trying to regenerate frozen Siberian mammoths.

In our lifetimes people may only learn about dinosaurs by studying their fossilized bones. A lot has been learned in the 150 years that scientists have been learning to identify dinosaur bones.

The Long Road to "Jurassic Park"

For centuries workers digging in quarries or peat bogs and farmers plowing their fields have brought up dinosaur bones from the ground. But for a long time, no one knew where the big bones had come from. A lot of people thought they were the bones of giants that had lived long ago. (Of course, the bones HAD come from giants! But the giants were animals, not humans.)

As science became more advanced, so did people's understanding of the dinosaurs. An 18th-century Frenchman named Georges Cuvier, who is considered to be the first paleontologist, understood what the fossilized "reptile" bones were. He examined an enormous jawbone and concluded that it had belonged to a huge sea lizard, later known as monasaur.

Entire dinosaur skeletons were rare, so it wasn't unusual for a scientist to try to describe entire 40-foot-long animals by examining only a few of their huge teeth or bones.

Originally, scientists thought dinosaurs were large reptiles. Today, many believe they were not true reptiles, or at least not like the reptiles of today. Dinosaurs did not crawl close to the ground like modern turtles, snakes, or lizards. Many dinosaurs, we believe, could move quickly and were warm-blooded like today's mammals and birds. At least some dinosaurs were nurturing parents (caring for their young in the nest), which is not true of today's reptiles. But, although it may be inaccurate, dinosaurs are still classed as reptiles because of their reptile-like skulls. Recently some scientists have suggested that dinosaurs be removed from the class *Reptilia* and put in a separate class called *Dinosauria* or *Archosauria*.

In the early 19th century, scientists began to identify and describe dinosaurs and write books about them. William Buckland, an Englishman from Oxford University, wrote about "Megalosaurus or Great Fossil Lizard" in 1824. Three years later, Dr. Gideon Mantell, also English, described dinosaur teeth and bones he'd found. And suddenly, dinosaur discoveries began coming right and left.

In 1841, Dr. Richard Owen of the British Museum was the first to use the word *dinosaur* to describe the prehistoric creatures. The word distinguished fossil remains of the prehistoric creatures from those of modern reptiles. (*Dinosaur* means terrible lizard.) Dr. Owen also developed our idea of dinosaurs as huge and reptile-like.

In 1858, on the other side of the Atlantic, Dr. Joseph Leidy of Philadelphia was the first to assemble dozens of bone fragments into a complete dinosaur skeleton. The animal he rebuilt was a hadrosaur, or duck-billed dinosaur, that had been found in New Jersey. People swarmed to the museum where the huge creature was displayed.

Because of the display's popularity, major museums all over the East soon began hiring scientists and sending out fossil-hunting expeditions. During the 1870s and 1880s, dozens of dinosaur discoveries were made in Montana, Wyoming, Colorado, and Utah. The "bone rush" was on! Over a few years, hundreds of tons of fossilized bones were shipped to museums for reconstruction.

Because such reconstruction had rarely been done before, a lot of it was only guesswork. Early displays showed dinosaurs with their long and heavy tails dragging the ground or showed them standing on all fours. Now it's known that many dinosaurs held their tails off the ground for balance, like birds do, and walked upright on their hind legs. Paleontologists now believe that dinosaurs had much in common with the birds of today.

Much remains to be discovered about the nature of dinosaurs, but scientists do agree about certain things.

Dinosaurs lived during the Mesozoic Era 245 to 65 million years ago. For 135 million years, they were the dominant land animal; and, although they could swim, they spent most of their time on land. Fossils reveal that dinosaurs laid eggs and had scaly skin and generally large tails.

Scientists have identified about 500 different species of dinosaurs, ranging in size from that of a small chicken to huge nine-story-tall *Apatosaurus*.

Dinosaurs differed from today's reptiles in the structure of their skeletons. Unlike today's reptiles, they had special hip sockets, and some of their vertebrae were fused to help support their (often) immense weight. Because no dinosaur has been found in the flesh, we know little about their hearts, lungs, and other internal organs.

Dinosaurs were actually two kinds of animals, saurischians (so-risk-eeons), and ornithischians (or-ni-thísk-eeons). The two were very different but are believed to have evolved from reptilian ancestors called thecodonts.

The saurischians were lizard-hipped dinosaurs like *Tyrannosaurus rex* and included two-legged meat eaters and huge four-legged plant eaters. The ornithischians were bird-hipped dinosaurs like *Stegasaurus* and other armored, plated, and horned dinosaurs.

Everything we know about dinosaurs has been learned by examining their fossilized remains—which are, of course, limited. That's because fossilization of animals that lived a long time ago is a natural process, but it's also somewhat rare. In addition, it takes a long time for fossils to form, and conditions have to be just right.

First, the animal must die in a place where it will be quickly buried. Otherwise it will decompose or predators will destroy it, and no fossilization can take place. Bones survive longer than soft body tissue, which is why the fossil record of dinosaurs is mostly bones.

Second, the ground where the animal is buried must have water with dissolved minerals seeping through it. If more ground water is added, the mineral solution will be diluted and fossilization will be slowed. If the land dries out, the process could be stopped completely. It may seem surprising that in certain dry areas today, such as western Montana, huge numbers of fossilized dinosaur bones have been found. The reason? Water was present when the fossilization was taking place.

Third, because fossilization happens slowly, the grave site must remain undisturbed long enough for it to take place. Caves and sinkholes, swamps and stagnant ponds (where sediments on the bottom don't get stirred up) are all good places to find fossils.

A century ago, scientists spent a lot of time describing and classifying dinosaurs. But they gave little attention to whether the bones were found where the animals actually lived or if several bones found together even belonged to the same animal. So a lot of mistakes were made reconstructing dinosaurs and interpreting their behaviors.

Digs of Today

Now, paleontologists, who spend many hours in the field searching for fossils as well as working with them in laboratories, are interested in what happened to an animal's bones *after* it died. Were they disturbed, moved, or chewed by other animals? Did earthquakes or volcanoes shove them around? Were they pushed from their original location by floods? (Today, bones may be lost or destroyed altogether as bulldozers scrape the ground for new roads and buildings.)

Locating fossils is not an easy job. A good place to look is in shales and slates, which are made from small-grained particles that once were saturated with water and provided favorable conditions for fossilization. Another good place is where geologic uplifting or erosion has occurred, exposing millions of years of sediments. To help with the search for fossils, paleontologists, might use a special type of ground-penetrating radar. But finding the ancient bones is just the beginning!

Before work gets underway, the dig site must be divided into small, equal squares called a grid, so information about fossils collected can be recorded very specifically. The site must be surveyed, and a detailed map made. While paleontologists dig, they make careful notes about everything they find.

Each fossil site is different, and paleontologists know they'll deal with a whole new set of conditions every time they dig. Bones might be buried in soil or embedded in rock. They might be brought out easily or with great difficulty. In a wet climate, mudslides can quickly bury bones the paleontologists have exposed. In a dry climate, earth can be practically as hard as rock and just as difficult to dig.

Sometimes fossilized bones are fragile and can break if they're not properly protected before being brought out. In this case, they will need to be coated with special adhesives or with plaster casts like those doctors use on broken arms or legs.

Once safely out of the ground, fossils are carefully numbered before being packed for shipping to museums or laboratories. Once they've arrived, they get carefully cleaned and studied. Bones in less than excellent condition may be put in boxes for storage. Bones that are well preserved may be reconstructed into skeletons for museum displays. Sometimes, if a piece or two are missing, they can be recreated from plaster or some other material to fill in gaps.

Paleontologists' work might sometimes seem difficult and tedious, because they work in the field where it's hot and dry. Sometimes they turn up only a few bones, and then may spend years piecing a fragmented skeleton back together in the lab. But the work can also be a highly exciting and rewarding. Just imagine digging up a dinosaur that had never been heard of before or finding your very first bone fragment!

You Can Volunteer

Students and science teachers who would like to take part in this dig can apply to the Paleo Field School, which is offered by the Museum of the Rockies in Bozeman, Montana. All summer, campers, who stay a week and live in tipis, learn how to dig and preserve fossils. (Campers must be at least ten years old.) At the museum in Bozeman, about 150 miles away, visitors can watch much of the cleaning and reconstruction work.

The museum uses volunteers at other Montana sites. For information about volunteering or taking part in the Paleo Field School write:

Museum of the Rockies
Montana State University
Bozeman, Montana 59715
            Or call: Dig-a-Dino at 406-994-3170

Other museums that use volunteers for dinosaur-related work include:

Denver Museum of Natural History
2001 Colorado Boulevard
Denver, Colorado 80205-5798
            Or call: 303-370-6387

Cleveland Museum of Natural History
Wade Oval, University Circle
Cleveland, Ohio 44106
            Or call: 216-231-4600

New Mexico Museum of Natural History
Volunteer Programs
1801 Mountain Road, N.W., P.O. Box 7010
Albuquerque, New Mexico 87194-7010
            Or call: 505-841-8837

National Museum of Natural History
Volunteer Program
10th Street and Constitution Avenue, N.W.
Washington, DC 20560
            Or call: 202-357-1300

More volunteer opportunities to work with fossils are available through the Bureau of Land Management (BLM), which manages some fossil sites in western states. For information write:

Project Coordinator
U.S. Bureau of Land Management
1849 C Street, N.W.
Room 3615, Washington, DC 20240
            Or call: 202-208-5261

Dinosaur Discovery Expeditions offers students and their families the chance to vacation in Utah, Colorado, or Wyoming and work with scientists in the field. They can dig for dinosaur fossils, work in a paleontology lab, and assist paleontologists. Participants have dug up *Brontosaurus, Allosaurus* and *Stegosaurus* fossils on these expeditions. For information write:

Dinosaur Discovery Expeditions
Dinamation International Society
189-A Technology Drive
Irvine, California 92718
            Or call: 800-547-0503

COPYCAT PAGE

PALEO-PUZZLER

Find the 28 words below that relate to paleontology.

Do you know what all the words mean? You can find out by reading this issue of NatureScope or looking them up in the glossary.

```
Y N E S T S P I S S C Y S T F
S R S P O T A R E C I R T N O
O A U E B N L U L I O O N E S
T C O B A E E A I E Z T O D S
A I E C P M O S T N O A D U I
J S C M A G N O P T S R O T L
R S A U T A T N E I E O C S S
U A T E O R O I R S M B E C K
A R E S S F L D S T R A H I E
S U R U A S O G E T S L T E L
O J C M U I G A N I M A L N E
R O N S R E Y F I S S A L C T
D S U R U A S O L L A R L E O
A P J T S E X C A V A T I O N
H L I Z A R D B O N E S P A H
```

ALLOSAURUS	EXCAVATION	MUSEUM
ANIMAL	FOSSILS	NESTS
APATOSAURUS	FRAGMENTS	PALEONTOLOGY
BONES	HADROSAUR	REPTILES
BURY	JURASSIC	SCIENCE
CLASSIFY	LABORATORY	SCIENTIST
CRETACEOUS	LIZARD	SKELETON
DINOSAUR	MESOZOIC	STEGOSAURUS
EGGS		STUDENT
		THECODONTS
		TRICERATOPS

SUSPENDED ANIMATION

Visit a working fossil quarry where animals succumbed and were buried by a volcanic eruption that occurred several hundred miles away.

The rolling Nebraska hills, dotted with dark green trees in a distinctly western landscape, give little indication of the tragedy that took place here so long ago. But where the earth's top few layers have been meticulously peeled away—at Ashfall Fossil Beds State Historical Park—many animals are revealed, preserved intact and leaving no doubt that a sudden catastrophe took place here in some long-gone age.

The fossil beds, home 10 million years ago to a wide variety of mammals, is not a spot you'd likely be driving past on the highway and decide on impulse to visit. Nevertheless, in the first five months the park was open to the public, more than 38,000 visitors made it their destination, coming to see the fossilized remains of the ancient rhinos, camels, and horses displayed here *in situ* (in the ground as found). It is a lonely site, a land where life ended with a violent, massive storm that laid down layer upon layer of glassy volcanic ash from a far-away eruption. The animals died of both suffocation and starvation—their lungs filled with bits of ash that also covered their food supply.

Fossils of early animals have been found in the area since the 1920s. But the discovery of a complete rhino that led to major excavation at Ashfall happened by accident.

In 1971, Dr. Michael Voorhies of nearby Orchard, Nebraska, a paleontologist at the University of Nebraska's State Museum, had come home for a visit. As a child he had often hunted fossils and Indian arrowheads here. Finding these buried pieces of history had led Voorhies to his study of paleontology and to his work in the field. Wandering along what's now called Discovery Gully, he caught sight of a partially exposed rhino jawbone protruding from a dry hillside.

Wind and rain over the millennia had worn away some of the volcanic ash *matrix* (the natural material that encloses a fossil) that had, for 10 million years, encased the rhino.

Voorhies discovered that not only was the animal's jawbone buried here—its skeleton was complete, and six more fossilized rhino skeletons were here as well. He realized he had stumbled on a significant fossil site.

The National Geographic Society provided funding for excavation that continued over the next three years. Crews of six to 10 members spent entire summers unearthing the ancient beasts embedded in the rock-hard ash. In those three years, in an area the size of a basketball court, more than 200 complete fossilized skeletons were found—100 juvenile and adult rhinos, 50 horses (of five species), 20 llama-sized camels, three hefty giraffe camels, and 29 crowned cranes. All were removed to the University of Nebraska and today are in research collections at the state museum.

Windows to the Past

While the excavations were underway, local people, fascinated by what was going on, would flock to watch, eating picnic lunches while paleontologists and students chipped free the fossilized bones. This interest prompted Voorhies to open a fossil park where the public could see how the uncovering is done and how the whole process works.

In 1986 the Nebraska Game and Parks Foundation bought 360 acres to develop the state historic park. Ashfall opened to the public on June 1, 1991.

Visitors come first to the orientation center, where they see a few examples of excavated animals and plaques explaining the history of Ashfall. They move on to the Rhino Barn, a 32- by 64-foot shed that covers excavation in progress and shelters 20 individual rhinos, a couple of horses, and one camel, all of which will remain *in situ* rather than moved to research collections.

These two sites, the orientation center and the barn, open rare windows into the long-distant past and give visitors a superb look at the rhinos, three-toed horses, camels, cranes, turtles (which appear little different from today's painted water turtles), tortoises, and other creatures that clustered around a large watering hole in what is now Antelope County after a huge cloud of volcanic dust drifted in.

At least 300 animals died here as the result of a volcanic eruption at Bruneau-Jarbridge "eruptive center" in what is now southwest Idaho, many miles west of Ashfall. It's likely that there were thousands of prehistoric critters roaming the savanna-like plain, which greatly resembled the subtropical landscape of East Africa today. The animals preserved at Ashfall just happened to perish in a spot low enough that, when subsequent drifts of ash blew in, they were buried in it and their bones were not scattered.

Inside the barn, a score of animals lies in high relief, their skeletons displayed as they were buried—in the round. Throughout the summer of 1992 two preparators from the University of Nebraska and four students of paleontology carefully unearthed other animals interred here. Greg Brown was chief preparator.

Preparators are people who collect and prepare fossil material—gathering it, then removing the matrix from around it in the lab, and consolidating the fossils, hardening them with plastics.

Brown squats on a narrow walkway at the barn's north wall. He is working vigorously with a small steel chipping hammer, removing eight or so inches of rock-hard volcanic ash to reveal the layer of matrix that covers the fossilized bones. Sprawled before him and his assistant, Holly Paxson, a student at the University of Nebraska, are the barrel-shaped ribs and other bones of 20 prehistoric rhinos. Two small three-toed horses are also revealed, one of them in disarray, the other lying as perfectly and calmly on its side as though it were peacefully asleep, "as fine a three-toed as you'll find anywhere," Brown says.

Brown is working to reveal the only camel thus far found in this area. One long spindly camel leg is already showing. The other has apparently been chomped by a carnivore, probably a dog, and reveals "a textbook example of scavenged bones," Brown notes. The unscavenged leg bone displays evidence in the lumpy ridges running along its length of the severe lung disease that killed the camel. Brown guesses the camel had suffered anywhere between three weeks to three months before succumbing to the illness. He speculates that the large group of animals at the watering hole had been caught there attempting to get relief from the agonies they suffered as glassy ash tore at their lungs.

The ash probably displaced the watering hole that was here. The ash was like snow, blown by the wind, filling in low spots—and for the bodies to be so well preserved, it had to have happened within weeks of the animals' deaths. The bones, many of which indicate severe lung disease (bones can develop such a malady within a week of the onset of lung disease), are not completely fossilized. Outer bone layers are stone, but inner layers are still organic. If water containing the proper elements was allowed to continue percolating through the bones, it's possible they would become fully fossilized.

Inches below where Brown's hammer chips away at the *overburden* (material that covers useful geological materials) are the camel's head and the long neck Brown is working to reveal. He sets to work with a small-bladed scalpel and soft-bristled paint brush, carefully scraping matrix, sweeping it away with the brush. (The matrix is gathered into buckets and later dumped into a nearby gully; enough of it was examined under microscopes to determine there were no micro fossils in it.)

Brown unearths more and more of the camel's delicate neck bones, strung in a long arc. He says the animal appears to have been a juvenile long-neck camel. It would be some time before the entire animal can be revealed; its back lies under the north wall of the barn, and it could be several years before the barn walls are expanded, he says, noting with a smile that "paleontologists are patient folks."

As Brown works, Paxson scrapes carefully near one of the rhinos with her scalpel. She hits a small bump in the ash (which is much finer than that of Mount St. Helens, she says) and quickly brushes away matrix, hoping to find treasure. But the small lump, examined by Brown's knowledgeable eye, turns out to be a bit of sand kicked up from the watering hole's muddy bed by the rhino. Paxson has been more fortunate on other occasions, she says. Earlier this summer she found a horse's skull.

Near to where the two work stands a *hydrothermograph* (a device that records temperature and humidity). Thus far, the bones have shown no sensitivity to the air, but should a problem develop later, paleontologists have a detailed record of conditions and can make any necessary adaptations.

The Heap

Many of the skeletons found at Ashfall are preserved down to minute detail. About 20 animals with food remains inside their rib cages were found here. A crane, displayed at the orientation center, is seen to have had, for its last meal, a small lizard that lies partially digested inside its rib cage. Another remarkable find is the skull of a barrel-bodied rhino that reveals its final meal of needle grass caught between its tongue bones. Such finds provide information about the animals' diet as well as about plants that once lived here.

The arrangement of skeletons indicates the order in which the animals died. First to go were the birds and turtles. Ten feet of volcanic ash covered the animals, all found in the lowermost three or four feet. (The ash was later covered in turn by sandstone, sand, and gravel, with soil on top, and all of this overburden must be cut away before the ash can be explored.) Crane and pond turtle remains were found at the bottom of the heap.

Next to die were the medium-sized animals—the five types of horse and three types of camel, herbivores that depended for their sustenance on grasses and other plants growing on the ground. When the glassy ash blew in, covering the land, the animals would have pushed their muzzles through it in an attempt to forage—and gotten a double whammy of glassy ash into their lungs. (Carnivores, the creatures that survived longest after the disaster, would have only inhaled the ash from the air around them.)

The skull, jaws, and a foot of a baby camel from this intermediate layer are displayed here, as is the skull of one of the small horses, its brain case crushed between the jaws of a hyenalike bonecrushing bear dog. To date, no skeletons of these dogs have been recovered at Ashfall, but they have been excavated at Knox County, Nebraska, from similar age deposits, and paleontologists believe they will eventually be found here, too. Many of the smaller herbivores would have been scavenged by meat eaters, the bear dogs and saber-toothed cats, although thus far cats have not been unearthed here, either. All finds have been herbivores, with the exception of the cranes and turtles.

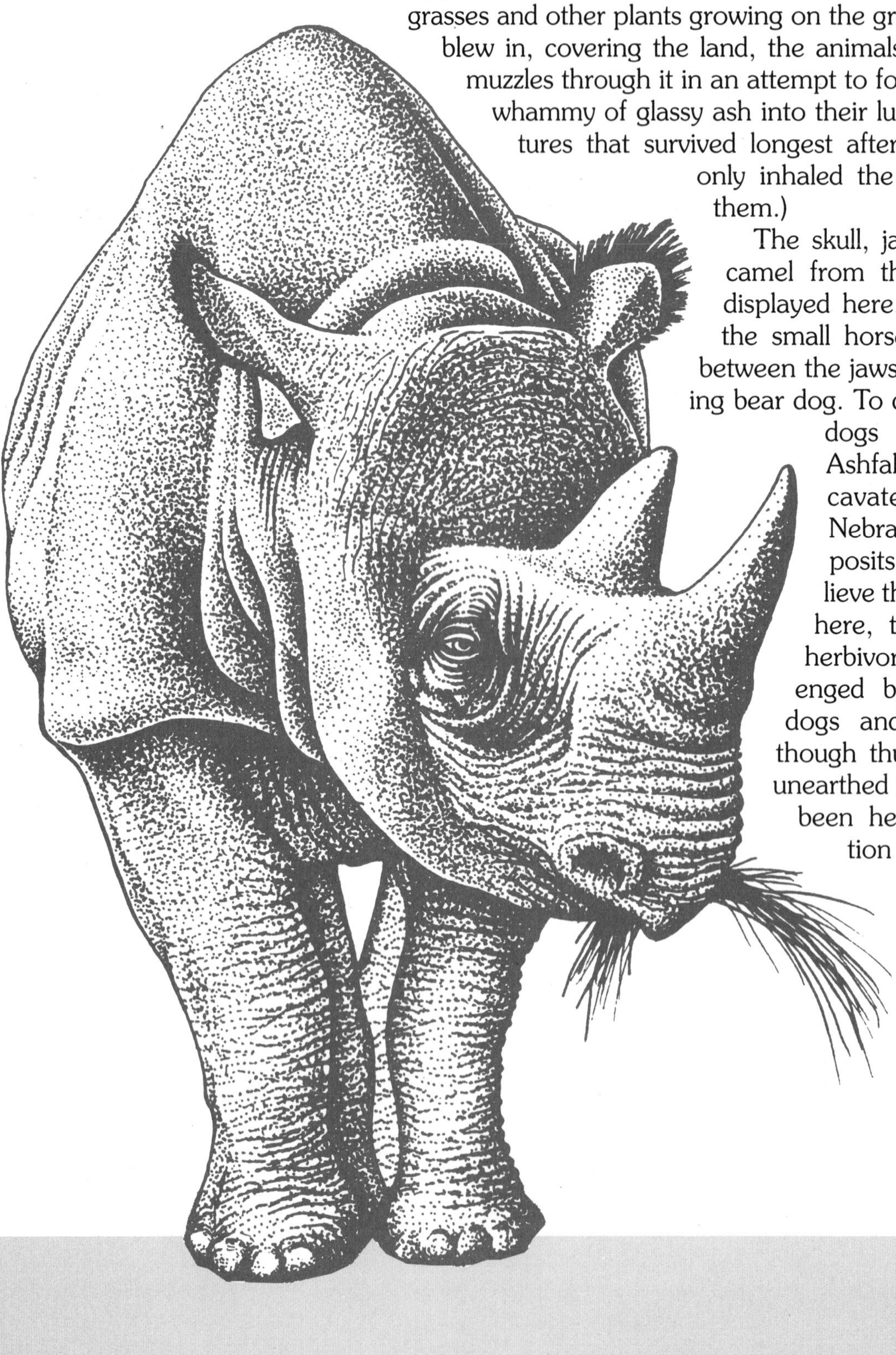

No land-dwelling dinosaurs will be found here. Because the area was covered during the dinosaur age (70 million years ago) by shallow marine seas, only marine animals will be found. Buried far below the Ashfall mammals, reptiles, and birds may lie mosasaurs (marine lizards), plesiosaurs (aquatic lizards), and pterodactyls.

The last animals to die here were the rhinos, 3,000-pound barrel-bodied animals built much like today's hippos. Among the more than 100 rhino skeletons found, only seven were adult males, easily differentiated from the females by the larger size of the tusks. The others were females and babies, many of them buried in the nursing position.

The Ashfall fossils provide a detailed look at wildlife of northeastern Nebraska at the time the ash blizzard took place. A mural painted on the orientation center's north wall depicts a world that closely resembled the savanna of East Africa: wild horses with stripes similar to the zebra, long-necked camels much like giraffes, rhinos, and elephants. In front of the mural stands the sturdy skeleton of a baby barrel-bodied rhino, one of 48 collected.

Visitors who would like a closer look at the plants and animals that once lived here can peer into a microscope that magnifies volcanic ash and fossils 500 times. Slides contain glassy ash taken from a rhino skeleton; diatoms, one-celled algae that live in water; ancient plants—bits of seeds and stems indicate grasses and rushes were growing here when the ash fell; and for comparison, ash spewed from Mount St. Helens during its May, 1980, eruption. The 1980 event was much smaller than the eruption that created Ashfall—presently the Ashfall ashbed extends from the Nebraska panhandle east across South Dakota to northeast Nebraska. East of Ashfall, glacier activity later removed the ashbed; west of the panhandle, the uplift that occurred during creation of the Rocky Mountains similarly destroyed the ash.

Don't Miss It!

To get to Ashfall, drive two miles west of Royal, Nebraska, on U.S. Highway 20 and watch for a sign to the site. Turn right (north) and drive six miles to the park. For information write: Ashfall Fossil Beds State Historical Park, P.O. Box 66, Royal, Nebraska 68773, or call 402-893-2000.

DIG THOSE DINOS!

To some, it might seem an unusual vacation—digging for dinosaur bones under a blazing summer sun, sleeping and eating in a Blackfeet style tipi. But people do it at a field school in Montana. Why? The story is the stuff of which movies are made.

In fact, Michael Crichton, in his 1990 best-selling book, *Jurassic Park,* which was made into the movie, patterned his hero after Dr. Jack Horner, and portions of the plot seem to have been inspired by Horner's real life story in Montana. That story begins in 1978, when Marion Brandvold, owner of a rock shop in Bynum, Montana, was out walking with her son and daughter-in-law in the Willow Creek Anticline, a badlands "wrinkle" in the dry and desolate rock formations of western Montana. They were searching for unusual rocks for the shop and found some large fossilized bones. Brandvold, believing them to be dinosaur bones, called Jack Horner, then a research scientist working as a preparator of fossils at Princeton University in New Jersey.

Horner identified the bones as the femur and jawbone of a duck-billed hadrosaur, a dinosaur that lived in the area about 80 million years ago. Then Brandvold nonchalantly showed him a coffee can full of small fossil bones that

turned out to be four baby dinosaurs. Brandvold led an ecstatic Horner to the discovery site near Choteau, and there he found much more—the nests where the babies had lived.

In the nests containing the small bones, Horner believed, lay the key to a totally new concept in dinosaur behavior. Promoting his theories, Horner became a pioneer in interpreting the animals' social behavior. He says, "I don't care how they died—I want to know how they lived." Hoping to find out, Horner commenced a major excavation at the Choteau site.

In 1979, Fran Tannenbaum, a member of Horner's team and a geology student at Princeton University, made yet another exciting discovery. Tired one evening after a day of excavating, she took a shortcut back to camp, and along the way practically stumbled over a fossilized dinosaur egg. She hurried to camp and returned to the egg site with a crew to investigate—on that first occasion they found 11 more dinosaur eggs, plus the skeletal remains of dinosaurs and an assortment of fossilized teeth. Because of the rich array of fossils buried there, the place came to be called Egg Mountain.

The dinosaur remains found there included those belonging to a small, spry herbivore Horner dubbed *Orodromeus makelai*. The *makelai* was for Horner's associate, Bob Makela, and *Orodromeus* means "mountain runner."

The fossilized eggs included those of yet another dinosaur, *Troodon*, a small carnivore that laid its eggs at the edges of nest sites of other species to assure its own young had plenty to eat.

Maiasaura means "good mother lizard," and Horner called a duck-billed hadrosaur eventually found on the site *Maiasaura peeblesorum*. Peeblesorum is in honor of John and James Peebles, owners of the land, who permitted the dig to continue until 1984.

The Nature Conservancy then purchased the site, which is only two square miles, and agreed to manage it in cooperation with the Museum of the Rockies. Plans were immediately underway to make the site scientifically meaningful without destroying it.

Today, excavation at the site moves at a glacial and intensely careful pace. It is now believed that at least 10,000 *Maiasaura* died and were washed here, probably in a mud flow.

Week-long courses start at the Museum of the Rockies in Bozeman, Montana. There, excellent exhibits at Phyllis B. Berger Dinosaur Hall provide a window into the past, back 80 million years. The displays also detail Horner's findings and how he arrived at his theories.

Camp-osaur

The Choteau dig lies about 12 miles southwest of town off a gravel road that coils up into mud-colored hills like a white serpent. There are no trees, and the summer sun blasts down on the high Montana plains. The jagged peaks of purple mountains are somber on far horizons.

Camp-osaur is a windblown expanse of dust reclaimed from the sagebrush and prickly pear-strewn desert. Students, including science teachers from around the country, instructed by a staff of 12, live and attend classes in the Camp-osaur tipis, the biggest of which can hold 50. Everything at the camp is portable, including showers that use sun-warmed water, and all must be toted out when camp ends each year—nothing is left that could possibly damage the desert ecosystem.

Great effort is made to create a hospitable environment, but there's little protection against sun or wind. Still, any physical discomfort is made trivial by the presence of dinosaur bones lying on the hillside nearby.

Dense layers of sediment, 1,000 feet or more, were cut away by glacial activity 1,000 years ago, leaving bones near or protruding from the surface. This isn't the case at Egg Mountain, where eggshells were occasionally seen a century ago but always misidentified as turtle shells. Diggers must work on a 40-foot rock face made of vitrified mud stone. At Camp-osaur ice picks and similar devices are sufficient; Egg Mountain is a microsite where only the most delicate tools and procedures are employed. To take out a nest, diggers usually remove about a ton of solid-block matrix. The matrix, however, is not bonded tightly to the eggshells.

Computer technology and CAT scans are quickly helping to build paleontological knowledge. For instance: Hadrosaurs grew from embryo to adult, increasing some 3,000 percent in only four years, evidence they were warm-blooded. They were equipped with something that stopped their growth and reduced their metabolism at maturity. (Cold-blooded, reptiles continue to grow throughout their lifetime.) It's also believed the *Maiasaurus* evolved quickly; evolution is generally a slow process but one that can be accelerated in times of stress. In the case of these dinosaurs, stress occurred as the Inland Seaway expanded on one side, and the Rockies grew up on the other, constantly shrinking their habitat (see "Why Here?"). To date, no one knows if *Maiasaurus* migrated, but they were *ubiquitous* (widespread), the cattle of the Cretaceous (or height of the Mesozoic Era).

Soon the micro screening of excavation sites, the systematic study as to what constituted the environment, will begin. Already, fossilized fish, turtles, and mollusks have been found.

In the past, as dinosaurs were discovered "a tooth here, a tooth there," it was difficult to tell if all the teeth belonged to the same animal. Now, a computer system developed to determine circulation patterns has also revealed that animals add a micro layer to their teeth each day of life.

So far, no genetic material has been found here, and it never will be because the area is too well cooked by volcanoes, but it's possible some may be retrieved elsewhere, shedding further light on hadrosaur life.

But overall, for learning how to recognize the various bones, and how to dissect bone beds, and for gleaning information about the social behavior of these animals, this has proven to be one of the world's greatest sites.

Dinosaur Jackets

Every fossil is jacketed and sent to Bozeman. Staff member Carole DeFord, who during the winter months is curator of the Cranbrook Institute of Science near Detroit, and several of her students outfit a *Maiasaura* tibia with a plaster jacket for its trip. The bone had been uncovered the day before and lay on the hillside, still tight in the ground, bleaching in the sun.

DeFord swaddles the long bone in water-soaked paper towels, which she then covers with strips of burlap that have been dipped into a thick solution of plaster of Paris and water. Afterward more soft plaster is smeared thickly over all, reaching as far underneath as possible, to make a "pedestal" for leverage.

In this land of blast-furnace sun and no humidity, a plaster jacket is fully dry and hard within three hours, but not considered "removable" for a full day. But another bone has been jacketed the day before, and is now ready to be broken free of its moorings.

DeFord kneels beside it, and holding tight to its pedestal, begins gently rocking it back and forth, then with a quick jerk, wrenches it free. Flipping it over, she and her students cover the bottom with more paper towels and plaster.

If a bone gets damaged during the process, its "integrity" can be restored by filling in gaps with Dextrin, a mix of cornstarch and plaster.

Ann Sutton, an invertebrate paleontologist from Medford, Oregon, who's a staffer here each summer, says, "This is a marvelous opportunity for learning, and for providing teachers with material to take back to their classrooms. An amazing amount of research is also going on here."

DeFord adds, "Students learn here that science is speculation based on educated guesses." They learn the scientific process: that a question gets things going, brainstorming yields possible answers, and is followed by testing of those answers, formulating more tests, drawing conclusions, and finally, by recording results. Most importantly, results must be shared.

"This is a wonderful, wonderful place," she adds. "Anybody who's ever loved dinosaurs and dreamed of knowing them first-hand can come here and do it—for me, this is a dream come true."

Why Here?

The dinosaurs studied near Choteau, Montana, were preserved because a specific set of circumstances occurred. The region, 500 million years ago, was a flat plain flooded periodically by shallow seas. By the end of the age of dinosaurs, the flooding had deposited thousands of feet of sediment.

Eventually the sediment was lifted up and folded to form the Rocky Mountains. Dinosaurs lived in the uplands and lowlands, and marine reptiles lived in the seaway. Sedimentation that accumulated in the seaway promoted fossilization. As the mountains were building, there was much volcanic activity, so it's possible that a volcanic blast from far to the west (in today's Idaho) killed great numbers of dinosaurs. The animals, embryos, and babies in nests, as well as adults, seem to have all died about the same time, possibly from gas or ash spewed out of a volcano. The dinosaur remains were fossilized where they lay and later swept away by volcanic mud flows to the Willow Creek Anticline.

A CISTERN TO THE CRETACEOUS

Answers to puzzling questions sometimes come from unexpected sources. For example, who would guess that a turtle stepped on by something huge 70 million years ago could help scientists understand what life was like during the age of dinosaurs?

But the fossil remains of a large turtle called *Adocus punctatus*, found recently at the Chronister Dig Project in eastern Missouri are doing just that—providing answers. Paleontologists believe the two-foot-long turtle was stepped on and squashed by an enormous dinosaur, a 40-foot-long, duck-billed hadrosaur.

Scientists have learned from studying the turtle's remains that it lived in water and believe that the animal inhabited a watering hole where dinosaurs came to drink. A hadrosaur migrating through the area probably accidentally stepped on the turtle, crushing it into the soft clay at the bottom of the pool.

Millions of years later, scientists hoping to learn about animals living there during the age of dinosaurs are digging carefully with shovels and trowels, and are unearthing treasure—hundreds of well-preserved bones that help tell the story.

The first dinosaur-age bones were found here completely by accident about half a century ago by a farmer named Oley Chronister, who was digging a hole for a cistern outside his house. Oley's mother, Lulu, had bought the 100-acre farm about 30 miles west of Cape Girardeau, Missouri, at the turn of the century. For 40 years, the family dipped water from a nearby stream and carried it to their house in buckets. But by 1941, Oley wanted a more convenient water source and began to dig the cistern.

He had gotten down about 15 feet when his shovel turned up something very unusual—a row of 15 bones that looked like they might be part of the tail of a very large animal. Oley couldn't even guess what it might have been because, until then, no dinosaur remains had ever been found in Missouri.

Oley's neighbors learned of the strange bones and soon word spread to the state capital, Jefferson City. The state geologist was sent down for a look. After carefully studying the three-foot length of bones that Oley had pieced back together, the geologist concluded they were "caudal vertebrae," tailbones from a dinosaur that had lived there during the Cretaceous period, 200 million to 65 million years ago. This came as quite a surprise to the scientific community, which had long believed that only three or four small pockets of Cretaceous soil were left in Missouri and that none of them contained dinosaur remains!

Geologists think that most of the rock formations in Missouri are much older than Cretaceous, going back 2 billion years to the Precambrian era or, at the very least 315 million years to the Pennsylvanian period. As the Rocky Mountains were being formed, about 70 million years ago, the land there and elsewhere in the Midwest was uplifted, leaving the most recently laid down Cretaceous soil exposed to the elements. Wind and rain slowly weathered most of it away, carrying it off to the *embayment*, or Gulf of Mexico, which back then lapped against the southern edge of Missouri. In fact, the Gulf of Mexico stopped about 40 miles short of where the Chronister Dig Project is located.

Today, this is a land of steep rolling hills where slender oak trees, hickories, walnuts, and a variety of bushes grow. The hills and valleys are crisscrossed by small, fast-flowing streams. But 65 million years ago, eastern Missouri looked like the Serengeti in East Africa looks today. High dolomite cliffs rimmed wide valleys where significant rivers flowed. Earthquakes were common, raising and lowering the land over its fractured crust many times.

The trees growing in Missouri now are different from those the dinosaurs nibbled on or sought for shade. There were birches with white, crinkly bark; ginkgos with leaves shaped like yellow fans; and metasequoias, relatives of the bald cypress.

Scientists believe that in Cretaceous times, herds of dinosaurs called hadrosaurs migrated through these valleys. They were named hadrosaurs, which in Greek means "big lizard," because of their enormous size. The animals had unusual long, flat snouts that looked like a duck's beak and a crest on top of their head. They were *bipedal* (meaning they walked on two legs), and they used their long tails for balance.

The hadrosaurs' breeding grounds were probably located on coastal plains near the Gulf of Mexico not too many miles away. When breeding season ended, the two-story-house-size dinosaurs would have lum-

Paleontologist Matt Forir of St. Louis prepares a pedestal or excavated ball of clay containing fossils for removal from the Chronister dig site in southeastern Missouri.

bered north a few dozen miles to feed. As they passed through the valley that the Chronister farm would occupy millions of years later, they would have stopped to drink at watering holes.

There, they would have met local residents, mostly reptiles. These would have included *Adocus punctatus*; another large species of turtle called *Naomicheleys*, or beaded turtle, and a species of crocodile called *Goniopholids*. These monstrous crocodiles were three or four times larger than the crocodiles of today, and scientists believe they were even fiercer predators than huge *Tyrannosaurus rex* (and everybody knows how fierce IT was). The crocodiles, which were as big as flatbed trailers, would have lain in wait for hadrosaurs to stop by for a drink, then pounced on the unsuspecting dinosaurs.

Scientists have concluded, from the broken-off tips of serrated crocodiles teeth found at the site, that the crocodiles also ate the turtles that shared their watering hole. The turtles' shells were thick and hard, more like the tortoises of today, and no doubt cost many a crocodile its teeth (though not for long, because crocodile teeth *regenerate*, or grow back).

Scientists who study crocodiles say that, except for being smaller now, crocodiles have not changed much in 235 million years. The same is true of turtles. *Adocus punctatus* was larger than today's soft-shelled turtle, but it looked very much the same. Like the water turtles of today, *Adocus* probably ate water plants, fish, and insects and may have come out of the water only long enough to lay eggs.

The most recent discovery at the Chronister dig, a football-size chunk of clay full of bones that included nearly half the remains of an *Adocus* and many of its claws, has confirmed scientists' belief that *Adocus* was a water turtle. The clue was in the claws. Like today's water turtles, *Adocus'* claws were long and straight. Turtles that live on land have sturdier, curved claws for easier walking. The stout legs and heavy claws of a land turtle would have made swimming difficult.

Paleontologists have known about the site for many decades, but interest in it has increased greatly over the past four or five years. This is mainly due to the efforts of a few scientists who have realized its value. Noted paleontologists around the country have called the Chronister site a "porthole into the Cretaceous." Nowhere else in the Midwest can scientists learn so much about life at that time.

The property with the dig site no longer belongs to Oley Chronister (who, by the way, never got his cistern—the rock underground was so fractured it wouldn't hold water!). Oley put his farm up for sale about 15 years ago, and 60 acres were bought by a geologist who had taken part in fossil digs there and was intrigued by the land's unusual rock formations.

Since most Missouri Cretaceous soil was weathered away, and the few pockets that remain are all located in one Missouri county, they are widely separated geographically from the Cretaceous soil found in other parts of the country. So scientists believe that the soil in Missouri might be different from Cretaceous soil elsewhere.

Were the *Adocus punctatus* turtles found at the Chronister site also different from *Adocus* found in other parts of the country, or might they even represent a new species? So far, scientific excavations have found *Adocus* remains in New Mexico, Montana, and New Jersey, all sites associated with the Cretaceous period.

As more complete remains are found—such as the most recent bonanza at the Chronister dig—better comparisons can be made. Imagine, a humble turtle helping unravel mysteries that scientists have wondered about for a century or more!

The *Adocus* remains found at the Missouri site may also provide answers to a far bigger question: What happened to kill off all the dinosaurs?

Some scientists believe that about 65 million years ago, a huge asteroid collided with the earth, sending up a dust cloud that would have taken years to settle back down. During that time, conditions on earth would have been similar to a nuclear winter, with no sunshine falling on the land. Since plants and animals can't live without sunlight, it wouldn't have taken too many years for everything to die.

However—and here lies the big dilemma—not all the animals died. Among the animals that survived was *Adocus punctatus*, which is known to

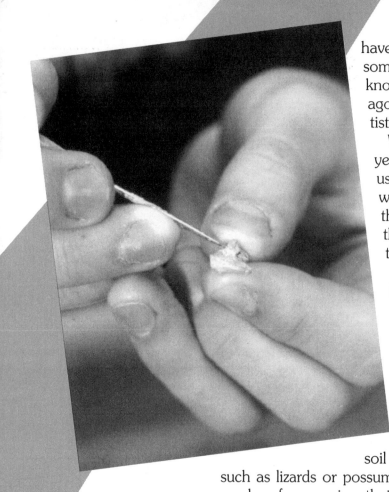

Forir cleans mud, from the bottom of a 70-million-year-old pond, to examine a rare claw from an Adocus *turtle. The size and shape of claws can tell scientists a great deal about how an animal lived. Can you think of anything you can tell about an animal by studying its claws?*

have crossed the *KT (Cretaceous-Tertiary) Boundary* in some parts of the country, surviving into the epoch known as the Eocene, until about 50 million years ago—long after the dinosaurs were gone. Then, scientists believe, these turtles died out from loss of habitat.

Whether *Adocus* lived in Missouri that long is not yet known, though it could be known soon. Scientists use a method of "washing" soil with acid to find out what plants pollen might be present (you can't tell it's there just by looking), and this enables them to date the soil. This type of testing is currently underway at the Chronister site.

If *Adocus* is found to have crossed the KT Boundary in Missouri, that information may raise as many questions as it answers. If *Adocus* could live on, is the asteroid hypothesis true? Turtles, which are very sensitive to temperature change, could have survived for a time by hibernating, but not for years!

Some paleontologists believe other animal species may have lived near the Cretaceous watering hole in Missouri, too. Screen-washing the soil may one day turn up small bones from creatures such as lizards or possum-like mammals and other marsupials (animals with pouches for carrying their young). It's also possible that winged dinosaurs known as pterosaurs (flying lizards), cruised overhead. These animals, with hollow bones and a 35-foot wingspan, were as big as a good-sized airplane.

It *is* known for certain that beaded turtles, animals that first appeared on earth during the Jurassic period, lived at the watering hole. The beaded turtle, *Naomicheleys*, was, at about three feet long, somewhat larger than *Adocus*. It had a higher-domed *carapace* (upper shell), indicating that it probably spent more time on land. The turtle's garnet-colored shell was crusted with a mosaic of tiny structures resembling beads. The beads may have helped protect the animal against predators.

The turtle was also equipped with thimble-sized dermal spikes made of bone that stuck out from the flesh on its hindquarters. The cone-shaped spikes probably served to protect soft flesh where the upper and lower shells didn't quite come together.

Paleontologists believe the Chronister site is important as a window into the Cretaceous period and that bones unearthed there may provide answers to a lot of questions. Some even think information gained from the fossils could completely change scientific thinking as to what life was like so long ago.

INFORMATION FOR THIS STORY WAS PROVIDED BY:
Bakker, Robert, paleontologist, Tate Museum at the University of Wyoming, Casper, Wyoming.
Brochu, Christopher, paleontologist, University of Texas, Austin, Texas.
Forir, Matthew, paleontology student, preparator, lab technician, instructor, Florissant Valley Community College, St. Louis, MO.
Stinchcomb, Bruce, geology professor, Florissant Valley Community College, St. Louis, MO.

SCIENTIFIC SEARCH

Find the 28 words below that relate to the Chronister Dig.

ASTEROID
BALE
BIPEDAL
BONES
CARAPACE
CHRONISTER
CLAY
CLAWS
CRETACEOUS
CROCODILE
DINOSAUR
EMBAYMENT
GEOLOGIST
HADROSAUR
MIGRATE
NAOMICHELEYS
PALEONTOLOGIST
PORTHOLE
PRECAMBRIAN
REMAINS
SANDSTONE
SCIENTIST
SITE
SOIL
SPECIES
SPIKE
TURTLE
VERTEBRAE

```
E T V E R T E B R A E Z A R R
C E S U O E C A T E R C E E U
A A R I G T U R T L E S T M A
P S M U G E Z R U F D S A B S
A D Y E A O O T A I I P R A O
R I A E L S L L N E E G Y N
A O L K L O O O O A N C I M I
C R C I O E H R T G D I M E D
L E E P B P H T D N I E G N D
A T T S O C R C R A O S P T E
W S N I A M E R I O H E T I R
S A N D S T O N E M P E L A B
S O I L E L I D O C O R C A R
G D P R E C A M B R I A N E P
I S C I E N T I S T B O N E S
```

Dinosaur Bibliography

Note: A * at the end of a listing indicates that a book is a good source of dinosaur pictures.

REFERENCE

Digging Dinosaurs by John R. Horner and James Gorman. Workman Publishing, NY, 1988.

Digging Up Tyrannosaurus Rex by John R. Horner and Don Lessem. Crown Publishers, Inc., NY, 1992.

Dinosaur by David Norman, Ph.D. and Angela Milner, Ph.D. (Dorling Kindersley, 1989)*

Dinosaurs by The Nature Company Discoveries Library (Time-Life, 1995)*

Dinosaurs: The Fossil Hunters by Dougal Dixon. Davidson Titles, Inc. Jackson, Tennessee, 1994.

Dinosaur Worlds: New Dinosaurs, New Discoveries by Don Lessem (Boyds Mills Press, 1996)*

Tracking Dinosaurs: A New Look at the Ancient World by Martin Lockley (Cambridge University Press, 1991)

Discovering Dinosaurs in the American Museum of Natural History by Mark A. Norell, Eugene S. Gaffney, and Lowell Dingus (Knopf, 1995)

The Illustrated Encyclopedia of Dinosaurs by David Norman (Random House, 1985)

Jurassic Park by Michael Crichton (Alfred A. Knopf, NY, 1993)

"Lessons from Leavings" by Karen Chin (***Natural History Magazine*** 6/95)

"The New Illustrated Dinosaur Dictionary" by Helen Roney Sattler (Lothrop 1990)

FIELD GUIDES

A Field Guide to Dinosaurs by David Lambert (Avon Books, 1983)

Fossil Collector's Handbook by Gerhard Lichter (Sterling, 1993)*

An Illustrated Guide to Fossils by Chris Pellant (The Nature Company, 1996)*

A Nature Company Guide: Rocks and Fossils by Arthur B. Busby III, Robert R. Coenraads, Paul Willis, and David Roots (Time-Life, 1996)*

Peterson First Guides: Dinosaurs by John C. Kricher (Houghton Mifflin, 1990)

ABOUT FOSSILS

Fossil by Paul D. Taylor, Ph.D. (Dorling Kindersley, 1990). All ages*

Fossils by Douglas Palmer (Dorling Kindersley, 1996). Intermediate and Advanced*

Fossils: A Guide to Prehistoric Life by Frank H.T. Rhodes (Golden Press, 1962). Advanced

CHILDREN'S BOOKS

Baby Dinosaurs by Helen Roney Sattler (Lothrop, Lee, and Shepard Books, 1984). Primary

The Big Book of Dinosaurs: A First Book for Young Children by Angela Wilkes (Dorling Kindersley, 1994). Primary*

***Bones, Bones, Dinosaur Bone*s** by Byron Barton (Crowell, 1990). Primary

Death From Space: What Killed the Dinosaurs? by Alexander Asimov (Gareth Stevens, 1994). Intermediate

Digging Up Dinosaurs by Aliki Brandenberg (Harper, 1988). Primary

The Dinosaur Encyclopedia: A Handbook for Dinosaur Enthusiasts of All Ages! by Michael Benton (Wanderer, 1984). Intermediate and Advanced

Dinosaur for a Day by Jim Murphy (Scholastic, 1992). Primary and Intermediate

Dinosaur Pop-Up ABC by Arlene Maguire (Simon & Schuster, 1995). Primary

The Dinosaur Question and Answer Book by Sylvia Funston (Little, Brown, 1992). Primary and Intermediate

Dinosaur Skeletons and Other Prehistoric Animals by Jinny Johnson (Reader's Digest, 1995). All ages*

Dinosaurs by Mary Packard (Simon and Schuster, 1981). Intermediate

Dinosaurs in Your Backyard by William Mannetti (Atheneum, 1982). Intermediate and Advanced

Dinosaurs: Unearthing the Secrets of Ancient Bones by Don Nardo (Lucent, 1995). Advanced

A First Look at Dinosaurs by Joyce Hunt and Millicent E. Selsam (Walker and Company, 1982). Primary

Fossils by William Russell (Rourke, 1994). Primary

Fossils Tell of Long Ago by Aliki Brandenberg (Crowell, 1972). Primary and Intermediate

The Great Hunters: Meat-Eating Dinosaurs and Their World by James O. Farlow and Ralph E. Molnar (Watts, 1995). Intermediate and Advanced

If the Dinosaurs Came Back by Bernard Most (Harcourt Brace Jovanovich, 1984). Primary

A Look Inside Dinosaurs by Neil Clark, Ph.D. (Joshua Morris, 1995). Advanced

The Magic School Bus in the Time of the Dinosaurs by Joanna Cole (Scholastic, 1994). Primary and Intermediate

Prehistoric Life by Steve Parker (Dorling Kindersley, 1993). Intermediate and Advanced*

Ranger Rick's Science Spectacular: Digging for Dinosaurs by Melvin Berger, is part of the Science Spectacular series (Newbridge Communications, 1993). Primary and Intermediate. Call 1-800-347-7829 to subscribe to the series.

Tyrannosaurus Was a Beast (dinosaur poems) by Jack Prelutsky (Mulberry Books, 1988). Primary and Intermediate

The Visual Dictionary of Prehistoric Life (Dorling Kindersley, 1995). All ages*

FILMS, FILMSTRIPS, SLIDES AND VIDEOS

Dinosaurs: Those Big Boneheads! is a Bill Nye the Science Guy video (Disney). Available where videos are sold. Intermediate

The Dinosaurs is a four-part series from PBS Home Video. Titles include **The Monsters Emerge, Flesh on the Bones, The Nature of the Beast**, and **Death of the Dinosaur**. Available from PBS Video, 1320 Braddock Pl., Alexandria, VA 22314-1698. Advanced

National Geographic Society has several dinosaur titles. **Dinosaurs on Earth: Then and Now** (Intermediate) is a videodisc and **Dinosaurs: Then and Now** (Intermediate and Advanced) is a video. **Dinosaurs and Other Creature Features** is part of the Really Wild Animals series of videos for all ages. The video **Fossils: Clues to the Past** is appropriate for advanced students. **Dinosaurs: Giant Reptiles** (Primary) is a Wonders of Learning Kit containing a read-along cassette, 30 student booklets, activity sheets, and background information. **The Age of Dinosaurs** (Intermediate and Advanced), **Fossils: Traces of the Past** (Advanced), and **Plants and Animals of Long Ago** (Primary and Intermediate) are filmstrips with cassettes. **Dinosaurs of North America** is a poster illustrating dinosaurs during the Mesozoic era. In addition, many of National Geographic's television specials are also available on video. For catalogs and more information call 1-800-368-2728.

GAMES AND EDUCATIONAL TOYS

Dinosaur: An Interactive Guide to the Dinosaur World is a kit containing a book, timeline, model, and game. (Dorling Kindersley, 1994). Intermediate.

The Dinosaur Society in East Islip, New York, publishes the **"Everything Dinosaur Catalogue,"** which contains several educational games, including **Dinosaurs and Things**, a board game for two to four players (Primary and Intermediate); **Dinosaur Hunters!**, an interactive puzzle game that simulates an actual fossil dig (Intermediate and Advanced); **Tyranno Ex**, in which players learn about dinosaurs' struggle for survival (Advanced); and **Tyrannosaurus Rex**, an excavation kit that allows intermediate and advanced students to dig up a complete T. rex skeleton. The catalog also has an extensive selection of dinosaur books, models, replicas, and fossil castings. Call 1-800-346-6366 to receive a catalog.

Draw 50 Dinosaurs and Other Prehistoric Animals by L.J. Ames (Doubleday, Inc., 1985). Primary and Intermediate

More Dinosaurs! and Other Prehistoric Beasts: A Drawing Book by Michael Emberley (Little, Brown, 1992). Intermediate

Press-out Dinosaurs contains photographic press-outs with a background scene (Dorling Kindersley, 1993). Intermediate

Survival or Extinction: The Dinosaur Game is a board game for primary and intermediate children that comes with a teacher's guide for using the game in the classroom. Available from The Dinosaur Society. Call 1-800-346-6366.

The Ultimate Prehistoric Sticker Book contains stickers and facts. (Dorling Kindersley, 1994). Primary and Intermediate

COMPUTER AND ON-LINE RESOURCES

Dinosaurs and Vertebrate Paleontology Links contains information and links to numerous dinosaur sites on the Internet. Their address is http://denrl.igis.uiuc.edu.isgsroot/dinos/vertpaleo.html

Discovery Channel Online features many of the Discovery Channel's and The Learning Channel's programs, including several relating to dinosaurs. A special school area for teachers contains information on how to obtain videos and other educational materials. The address is http://www.discovery.com

Scholastic's **The Magic School Bus Explores in the Age of Dinosaurs** is a CD-ROM appropriate for Primary and Intermediate students. Covers the three periods when dinosaurs roamed the Earth. Students learn about dinosaurs by helping create a photo album for their teacher, Ms. Frizzle, and by playing games like a dinosaur skeleton puzzle. From Microsoft. Available where educational software is sold.

Smithsonian Institution Dinosaur Museum is a CD-ROM for Intermediate and Advanced students that features a wealth of information on dinosaurs from the Triassic, Jurassic, and Cretaceous periods. Users can view dinosaur skeletons, dioramas, and fossil finds. They can fit dinosaurs into a geologic timeline. Sound enables users to hear dinosaur "voices." Special segments allow users to learn about eminent paleontologists, view clips of classic dinosaur movies, explore the various theories of extinction, and dispel myths about dinosaurs. After exploring all the museum has to offer, kids can play a game to reinforce what they've learned. Available from Perspective Visuals, 4112 Fairfax St., Fairfax, VA 22030; 1-703-352-9315.

Smithsonian Online brings the resources of the Smithsonian Institution to teachers over the Internet. By accessing the Smithsonian's Web page, teachers can find materials specifically for elementary and secondary grades, including photos that can be downloaded and reprints of articles, including "Fossils of the Atlantic Coastal Plain" and "How Paleontologists Bring Dinosaurs Back to Life." The address for the Web page is http://www.si.edu/ The National Museum of Natural History has its own Web site: http://nmnhwww.si.edu/nmnhweb.html You can also access Smithsonian Online over America Online.

OTHER ACTIVITY SOURCES

American Educational Products offers several fossil teaching aids suitable for advanced students, including fossil collections, flash cards, books, videos, and lab kits. To obtain a catalog, call 1-800-446-8767.

Investigating Science With Dinosaurs by Craig A. Munsart (Teacher Ideas Press, 1993). Intermediate and Advanced

Janice Van Cleave's **Dinosaurs for Every Kid: Easy Activities That Make Learning Science Fun** (Wiley, 1994). Intermediate and Advanced

The Dinosaur Society publishes **The Dino Times**, a monthly newspaper for children, and **The Dinosaur Report**, a quarterly newsletter for adults. The Society also puts out a list of recommended books about dinosaurs and a catalog offering numerous materials, including **Wonderquest Dinosaur Picture Cards**, which contain 24 colorful cards complete with facts, skill building exercises, activities, and size comparisons (Intermediate); a 5-feet-long dinosaur timeline poster; and more. For more information and a catalog call 1-800-346-6366. Or visit their Web site at http://www.dinosociety.org

The Nature Company offers toys, books, videos, and more. Teacher's get a 15% discount on purchases in Nature Company stores. Call 1-800-227-1114 for a catalog.

WHERE TO GET MORE INFORMATION

- museums of Natural History
- departments of paleontology at local colleges and universities
- nature centers
- paleontology clubs

Internet Address Disclaimer
The Internet information provided here was correct, to the best of our knowledge, at the time of publication. It is important to remember, however, the dynamic nature of the Internet. Resources that are free and publicly available one day may require a fee or restrict access the next, and the location of items may change as menus and homepages are reorganized.

Natural Resources

Ranger Rick, *published by the National Wildlife Federation, is a monthly nature magazine for elementary-age children.*

Ranger Rick magazine is an excellent source of additional information and activities on dinosaurs and many other aspects of nature, outdoor adventure, and the environment. This 48-page award-winning monthly publication of the National Wildlife Federation is packed with the highest-quality color photos, illustrations, and both fiction and nonfiction articles. All factual information in **Ranger Rick** has been checked for accuracy by experts in the field. The articles, games, puzzles, photo-stories, crafts, and other features inform as well as entertain and can easily be adapted for classroom use. To order or for more information, call 1-800-588-1650.

The EarthSavers Club provides an excellent opportunity for you and your students to join thousands of others across the country in helping to improve our environment. Sponsored by Target Stores and the National Wildlife Federation, this program provides children aged 6 to 14 and their adult leaders with free copies of the award-winning **EarthSavers** newspaper and **Activity Guide** four times during the school year, along with a leader's handbook, EarthSavers Club certificate, and membership cards. For more information on how to join, call 1-703-790-4535 or write to EarthSavers; National Wildlife Federation; 8925 Leesburg Pike; Vienna, VA 22184.

ANSWERS TO COPYCAT PAGES:

WHAT DOESN'T BELONG? (p. 21)

WHO'S A DINOSAUR? (p. 12)

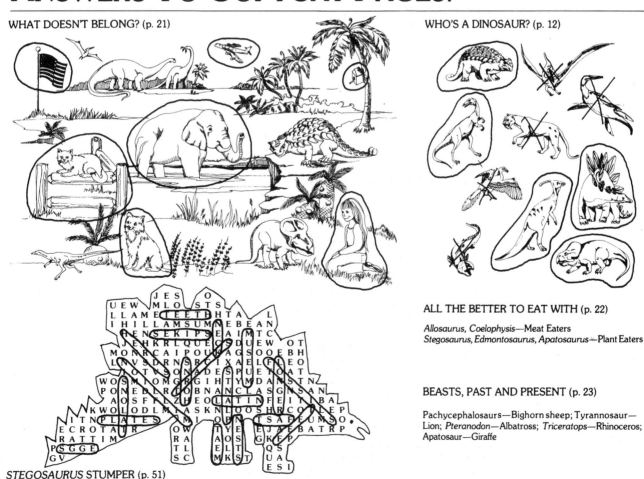

ALL THE BETTER TO EAT WITH (p. 22)

Allosaurus, Coelophysis—Meat Eaters
Stegosaurus, Edmontosaurus, Apatosaurus—Plant Eaters

BEASTS, PAST AND PRESENT (p. 23)

Pachycephalosaurs—Bighorn sheep; *Tyrannosaur*—Lion; *Pteranodon*—Albatross; *Triceratops*—Rhinoceros; *Apatosaur*—Giraffe

STEGOSAURUS STUMPER (p. 51)

1. teeth 2. eggs 3. fossils 4. neck 5. horns 6. tracks 7. plants 8. feet 9. plates 10. nests 11. talons 12. herds 13. spikes 14. longer 15. Latin 16. million 17. museum 18. fast 19. meat

Paleo-Puzzler Answers (p. 76)

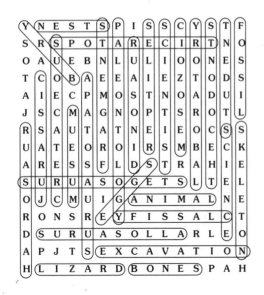

Scientific Search Answers (p. 91)

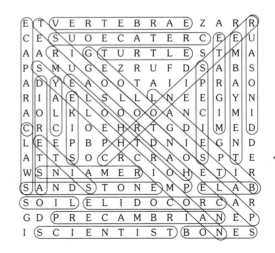

NORTH AMERICAN ANIMALS

Great Horned OWLS

by Christina Leaf

BLASTOFF!
3
READERS

BELLWETHER MEDIA • MINNEAPOLIS, MN

Note to Librarians, Teachers, and Parents:

Blastoff! Readers are carefully developed by literacy experts and combine standards-based content with developmentally appropriate text.

Level 1 provides the most support through repetition of high-frequency words, light text, predictable sentence patterns, and strong visual support.

Level 2 offers early readers a bit more challenge through varied simple sentences, increased text load, and less repetition of high-frequency words.

Level 3 advances early-fluent readers toward fluency through increased text and concept load, less reliance on visuals, longer sentences, and more literary language.

Level 4 builds reading stamina by providing more text per page, increased use of punctuation, greater variation in sentence patterns, and increasingly challenging vocabulary.

Level 5 encourages children to move from "learning to read" to "reading to learn" by providing even more text, varied writing styles, and less familiar topics.

Whichever book is right for your reader, Blastoff! Readers are the perfect books to build confidence and encourage a love of reading that will last a lifetime!

This edition first published in 2015 by Bellwether Media, Inc.

No part of this publication may be reproduced in whole or in part without written permission of the publisher. For information regarding permission, write to Bellwether Media, Inc., Attention: Permissions Department, 5357 Penn Avenue South, Minneapolis, MN 55419.

Library of Congress Cataloging-in-Publication Data

Leaf, Christina, author.
  Great Horned Owls / by Christina Leaf.
    pages cm. – (Blastoff! Readers. North American Animals)
  Includes bibliographical references and index.
  Summary: "Simple text and full-color photography introduce beginning readers to great horned owls. Developed by literacy experts for students in kindergarten through third grade"– Provided by publisher.
  Audience: Ages 5-8.
  Audience: K to grade 3.
  ISBN 978-1-62617-189-3 (hardcover : alk. paper)
  1. Great horned owl–Juvenile literature. I. Title.
QL696.S83L45 2015
598.9'7–dc23
                                                        2014041885

Printed in the United States of America, North Mankato, MN.

Table of Contents

Great horned owls are mighty **raptors**. These birds are common throughout all of North America except the northernmost parts of Canada and Alaska.

great horned owl range = ▢

conservation status: least concern

Extinct

Extinct in the Wild

Critically Endangered

Endangered

Vulnerable

Near Threatened

Least Concern

The owls usually live in forests. However, they can **adapt** to live in deserts, swamps, and even cities.

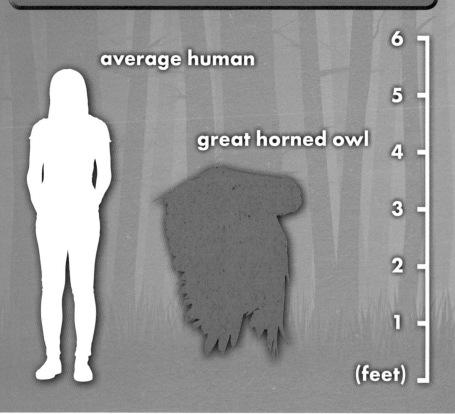

Size of a Great Horned Owl

average human

great horned owl

6

5

4

3

2

1

(feet)

Great horned owls are among the largest owls in North America.

Their bodies are about 2 feet (0.6 meters) long. Their wings can measure almost 5 feet (1.5 meters) across.

Great horned owls have **ear tufts** on their heads. These feathers look like horns.

The owls move them to **communicate** with family members. The ear tufts also make the owls look **threatening** to enemies.

Identify a Great Horned Owl

ear tufts   big, yellow eyes   hooked beak

Ear tufts help great horned owls blend in with trees while they sleep.

Brown, gray, and cream spotted bodies also hide the owls against tree bark.

Great horned owls usually search for food in the late evening and at night.

Large, yellow eyes help these **carnivores** spot **prey** in the dark. Excellent ears let the owls hear the smallest of sounds.

Great horned owls hunt from a **perch**. They turn their heads to look all around.

Then the birds dive down to catch dinner. Soft wing feathers make them silent fliers. They attack by surprise.

deer mice

skunks

cottontail rabbits

crows

gray squirrels

meadow voles

The owls' sharp **talons** grab prey. Favorite catches are small **mammals**. However, their strong grip can hold much heavier prey.

16

The owls tear apart larger prey with hooked beaks. They swallow smaller prey whole.

Nesting

Female great horned owls lay eggs in winter. They use empty nests built by other big birds.

Males bring food to the nests.
Females stay with the eggs to
keep them warm.

Baby Facts

Name for babies: owlets

Number of eggs laid: 1 to 4 eggs

Time spent in egg: 30 to 37 days

Time spent with parents: 6 to 7 months

Owlets stay with their parents
after they **hatch**. Mom and dad
protect the babies from danger.
They will attack any **predator**
that comes too close!

Glossary

adapt—to become comfortable with something

carnivores—animals that only eat meat

communicate—to share information and feelings

ear tufts—feathers on the heads of great horned owls; ear tufts are not actually used for hearing.

hatch—to break out of an egg

mammals—warm-blooded animals that have backbones and feed their young milk

owlets—baby great horned owls

perch—a high place from which a great horned owl can watch for prey

predator—an animal that hunts other animals for food

prey—animals that are hunted by other animals for food

raptors—large birds that hunt other animals; raptors have excellent eyesight and powerful talons.

talons—the strong, sharp claws of great horned owls and other raptors

threatening—scary, or likely to cause harm

To Learn More

AT THE LIBRARY

Bodden, Valerie. *Owls*. Mankato, Minn.: Creative Education, 2013.

Frankenhuyzen, Robbyn Smith van. *Adopted by an Owl: The True Story of Jackson the Owl*. Chelsea, Mich.: Sleeping Bear Press, 2001.

Frick, Ivi. *Hunting With Great Horned Owls*. New York, N.Y.: Gareth Stevens Pub., 2012.

ON THE WEB

Learning more about great horned owls is as easy as 1, 2, 3.

1. Go to www.factsurfer.com.

2. Enter "great horned owls" into the search box.

3. Click the "Surf" button and you will see a list of related web sites.

With factsurfer.com, finding more information is just a click away.

Index

The images in this book are reproduced through the courtesy of: gkuchera, front cover; mlorenz, pp. 4 (top), 10 (bottom); Vlada Z, p. 4 (bottom); Don Fink, pp. 6-7; Igor Kovalenko, p. 8; John Giustina/ Corbis, pp. 9-10; DnDavis, p. 10 (top left); Chris Hill, p. 10 (top center); Julie C. Wagner, p. 10 (top right); Cynthia Kidwell, p. 11; Alan Carey/ Corbis, p. 12 (top); Val Thoermer, p. 12 (bottom); Jack Nevitt, p. 13; artcphotos, p. 14; mallardg500/ Getty Images, p. 15; Close Encounters Photo, p. 16 (top left); Eric Isselee, p. 16 (top right, center right); Michael Chatt, p. 16 (center left); Michael Rowlandson, p. 16 (bottom left); Magnus Manske/ Wikipedia, p. 16 (bottom right); Anthony Mercieca/ Animals Animals, pp. 16-17; Minden Pictures/ SuperStock, pp. 18-19; Chris Kolaczan, p. 20; Ronnie Howard, pp. 20-21.